Teach•er ver•ance.

n. Nurturing Hope While Embracing **Perseverance** in Education

Dr. Jen Mott

Teacherverance

Nurturing Hope While Embracing Perseverance in Education

Dr. Jen Mott

Teacherverance: Nurturing Hope While Embracing Perseverance in Education

Dr. Jen Mott

Cover Design by: Carrie O'Neal

Copyright © 2024—Dr. Jen Mott, LLC Teacherverance
Reach out to Dr. Jen Mott for permission to use at www.DrJenMott.com

As an educator, the author knows Artificial Intelligence can add value to efficiency, productivity, and idea generation. It is worth noting, however, that this book was written entirely by a human as no Artificial Intelligence was used to help complete the project.

Disclaimer: The author makes no guarantees concerning the level of success you may experience by following the advice and strategies contained in this book, and you accept the risk that results will differ for each individual. The purpose of this book is to educate, entertain, and inspire.

This is based on an original academic study by the author titled, "Capturing Teacher Perseverance: A Study of Veteran Teachers Who Have Remained in the Classroom." If you're interested in the original research, read more here: http://rave.ohiolink.edu/etdc/view?acc_num=xulead1610034539065179

For more information: www.DrJenMott.com

ISBN: 979-8-9899933-0-7 (print)
ISBN: 979-8-9899933-1-4 (e-book)

Before you start...!

Visit www.DrJenMott.com/books/

(or use the QR code)

...for more books by Jen and for a FREE download with encouragement + a visual* of the main themes of this book!

*Print the visual for your desk, or share with a friend, and/or keep for your own reminder of how awesome you are.

Thanks for being here!

This book is dedicated to the *teachers* of this world. Whatever the content or grade level, wherever the school...*you* are a difference maker in this world, and we need you.

Teachers cannot do what they do without the support of professionals, administrative assistants, the custodians, the child nutrition workers, and the school administrators who help support the students in the building. To anyone who serves students daily in any capacity—this book is for you, as you are also a difference-maker in the lives of students and teachers.

Contents

Foreword

When I first heard the name Dr. Jen Mott, I was at a National Speakers Association conference in Orlando, Florida. A mutual friend who was helping me write an educational keynote said emphatically, "Tom, you *need* to know Jen Mott. She is extraordinary!" After one phone call, I could tell that Jen was not only an expert in her field, but she was also on a mission to help as many people as possible find what was extraordinary about themselves. She was my kind of teacher.

Many of the ideas Jen shared with me in that and subsequent conversations are the very ideas that comprise this book—and they are brilliant! In my early days as an elementary classroom teacher, I discovered the profound impact that captivating lessons and engaging experiences could have on students. It was clear that Jen shared the same philosophy, and I wondered how our minds clicked on so many levels. Then it became apparent.

Beyond educators—I am a magician. Jen is a juggler. Seriously.

Through our conversations, I found a kindred spirit in the fusion of education and performance. The art of juggling, much like magic, is a symphony of coordination, precision, and the relentless pursuit of mastery. In this book, Jen seamlessly weaves a narrative that not only explores why teachers today are leaving the profession in record numbers but also draws profound parallels to the multifaceted role of educators.

The magic of education, I realized, lies not just in the curriculum but in the ability to create an environment where learning becomes a captivating adventure. It is this same belief that has driven Jen to infuse her teaching with the artistry of performance and risk taking, providing a unique and enchanting perspective that resonates with students.

Allow me to take you on a brief detour into my own educational journey, a path paved with the enduring influences of my parents. My father, a dynamic and cutting-edge school principal, ignited my passion for education at a young age. His innovative approaches to learning and unwavering commitment to nurturing young minds set the stage for my own venture into the world of teaching. Equally influential was my mother, an early childhood music teacher whose teaching methodology transcended traditional boundaries. Through orchestrated music, rhythm, storytelling, and movement, she imparted lessons that resonated deep within. Her ability to infuse hope, empathy, and love into her lesson plans became the guiding light that shaped my belief in the power great teachers could have on their students.

In much the same way, Jen sheds light on what propels educators forward. It's a daunting task, however, in a profession where each day brings new challenges, uncertainties, and the delicate balancing act of multiple responsibilities. The message of *Teacherverance* is a crucial one for educators to adopt if they are to navigate these complexities with grace and determination.

Jen's theme of Higher Calling, defined by awe, spiritual awakening, and faith, mirrors the transcendent connection

I've always felt toward education. Like the teachers described in the book, my journey has been guided by a profound sense of purpose and a belief in a higher calling. The theme of Community, with its four pathways connecting teachers with students, colleagues, the broader community, and friends or mentors outside of school, reflects the interconnectedness that defines the heart of teaching. I am reminded of the magic that happens when we build meaningful relationships, not just within the classroom but also with the larger tapestry of the community.

What Jen calls the Only Option, in its dual nature of positive inspiration and pragmatic realism, strikes a chord close to my heart. Teaching is not merely a job; it is a vocation—an unwavering commitment, and a source of inspiration. It is the recognition that, despite challenges, there is no other role that captures the essence of our purpose as educators. Contextual Joy, the theme exploring the joy found in the right environment, school building, leadership team, or the students themselves, is at the core of moments I've experienced in my own educational journey. It is the joy that comes from aligning the right factors, creating an environment where learning becomes fearless and the learners become participants in the process. I am filled with gratitude to teach in such a district as Blind Brook, New York, where such ideals are fostered and promoted.

As you embark on this transformative journey through *Teacherverance*, I invite you to reflect on your own educational odyssey. Whether you are an educator, administrator, policymaker, or a passionate advocate for education, there is a thread within these pages that will resonate for you. Our collective stories shape the narrative of education, and it is through perseverance, community, and joy that we can truly make a lasting impact.

As educators, we are tasked with the awe-inspiring responsibility of shaping young minds, and Jen beautifully underscores the importance of infusing creativity, passion, and resilience into this endeavor. The message of teacher perseverance is not just a call to action; it is a testament to the indomitable spirit of educators.

I extend my deepest gratitude to Jen for crafting a work that not only delves into the challenges of teaching but also celebrates the resilience, dedication, and love that define the teaching profession. May this book inspire you to tap into your own teacherverance and approach our roles as educators with a sense of wonder and the belief that, indeed, the extraordinary is possible within the ordinary.

Tom Pesce

www.tompesce.com

@tompesceofficial

Info@tompesce.com

Introduction

It is December 2014. I am in my fourth full school year of teaching, and I am considering resigning. I have already experienced a "reduction in force" twice in two different school districts. To continue working at one point, I *needed* to switch content areas—as assigned by administration. I have had the curtain pulled back on teaching in ways I never expected—personally and professionally and played out on a larger stage through recent events that gripped the world's attention toward America's schools.

Enter Zach. He is in his second full school year of teaching, and for his own reasons, he is also considering resigning. He starts considering changing types of schools to see if a different environment gives him a better situation while trying to navigate being recently married and building a life around this newfound career. Zach starts connecting with other teachers and hearing their stories to understand more the unique needs teachers have and what he needs to consider for himself over the years as he continues.

Fast-forward to spring 2019, I am officially in the ABD—"all but dissertation"—phase of a doctoral program in Leadership Studies at Xavier University in Cincinnati, Ohio. As a full-time assistant principal and a part-time university professor, I had already chosen a topic for my dissertation research: teacher perseverance.

As someone who persevered through what I hope is my most challenging school year of my career in 2014, ever the optimist, I felt compelled to challenge the language in the education world saying that teachers were leaving and, consequently, the United States had a teacher shortage. I questioned why nobody was speaking with the teachers who were *staying*. Those who had given decades of their lives committed to building into young people. Those whom I was celebrating each May and June as they said goodbye to storied careers of more than thirty years. Educators, like my own parents and other family members, whom I had seen stay in such a difficult field while being asked to jump through increasingly more hoops year after year.

Also in 2019, Zach was figuring out his exit strategy, as he had now exhausted his options as a private, public, and charter schoolteacher and felt he needed to give his family more of his time and energy. He had tried different schools, grade levels, and content areas and still felt there was something missing in his life, and teaching was not giving him the life he hoped for or imagined. After seven years of teaching, he had navigated a health scare with his wife and a physical scare with his students, and both helped him come to terms with what was most important.

As Zach was determining what life after teaching looks like for him and his family, I worked with my dissertation committee to design a study to explore the relationship between self-assessed levels of veteran teacher grit and the stories those same teachers would tell as they reported factors contributing to their longevity in their roles. After four years attending classes on a set schedule in the doctoral program, spring 2019 brought newfound freedom, when I could work on this project whenever and wherever I chose. I focused on enjoying this extra time that year by traveling to ten countries on forty flights, all while working one full-time and a few part-time jobs. While this was an unforgettable experience, it naturally left me little time to gather the actual teachers I needed for the study I had designed yet had not started.

Enter spring 2020. Suddenly, I found myself during a global pandemic with a preconceived concept of interviewing veteran teachers, asking them why they had stayed in their chosen career at arguably one of the most confusing and unsettling times in the entire history of the field. My committee encouraged me to persevere by allowing me to set the bar lower than planned and hope for only twenty teachers. Surprisingly, as I started sharing news of the study, I quickly found myself with over forty willing and experienced teachers of grades six through twelve from southwestern Ohio who, at the time, had already remained in the classroom for at least fifteen consecutive years.

I will be forever grateful to the *forty-four* amazingly dedicated classroom teachers who volunteered their precious time to participate in this study. Any fall would be a challenging time for classroom teachers to engage in additional projects as they approached the end of the semester. However, fall 2020 proved to be the trickiest part of any school year we have had in our careers, and I still was able to gain permission from over forty teachers representing seven school districts. Their voice, on behalf of their peers, helped inform this entire book, and we will all be better for their time, efforts, and energy.

Classroom teachers are my personal heroes. They play an integral part in society. They not only shaped me as an early student-turned-educator but are also shaping every single member of the workforce today. They are on the front lines of the "people business" we call education, and it is imperative we give them the voice they deserve and look to them to help us lead with optimism, clarity, and innovation. Teachers, administrators, and all post-COVID-19 industry leaders who read this must recognize the importance of our work and the invaluable impact it can have on this world. Educators are fortunate to be in the business of *people*, as we get the chance daily to impact people's lives in unique, tangible, and meaningful ways.

May we all use this book and these stories to learn ways to harness *teacherverance* in our own communities and organizations to leverage the experience of veteran teachers to improve overall employee morale. May classroom teachers find this to be an encouragement, a gift, and validation as they consider ways to continue persevering in such a demanding, yet important, profession. Classroom teachers deserve to know they are surrounded by a society of people who are standing on their shoulders. And that—even as the challenges increase—we are all collectively grateful for the ones who persevere, while trying to hold out hope that the incredible teachers like Zach choose to stick it out for the sake of the students they serve. How do teachers spend their time after teaching? Better yet, are there factors that the teachers who do stay have in common that can be captured, replicated, or shared so teachers like Zach do not have to feel they must leave their originally chosen profession?

To help support teachers, this book has four parts. Part 1 will explore how we even got to where education is today and will answer the questions: How bad is the teacher shortage we keep hearing about, and what can be done to fix it? Part

2 will share the results of the study upon which this work is based and share the information behind the themes found. Then, readers will have the opportunity in part 3 to consider their own stories and respond to questions asking them to think more deeply about their own experiences around education. Part 4 will look ahead to what can be done, given what we have learned, and how we can all move forward with these themes in mind *and* try to make a better future for our educators—which will undoubtedly impact our students.

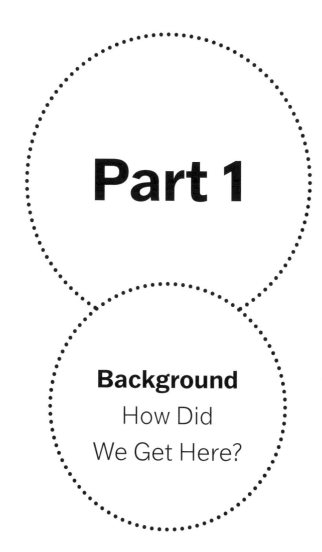

Part 1

Background
How Did
We Get Here?

Chapter 1
How Did We Get Here?

Each year schools nationwide must hire tens of thousands of teachers as a result of beginning and mid-career teachers leaving the profession.
Desiree Carver-Thomas & Linda Darling-Hammond, 2019

"Glorified babysitters": Teachers have been called this and many other degrading terms well before the COVID-19 pandemic. Anyone who is in education or related to an educator knows that this description far undermines the actual work educators put in daily to create unique, creative, and engaging lessons. While looking after their classrooms, teachers also manage various needs the students present, and they analyze data to help meet those needs and improve test scores and student well-being.

Even before the pandemic, there was plenty of research published about rising teacher demand as a function of changes in student enrollment, shifts in ratios, and high levels of teacher attrition.[1] While there are certainly statistics to support the fact that teacher attrition is a real issue, there is little focus on the other side, that of teacher retention, with an emphasis on *why* teachers *stay* in the field.

Before examining teacher retention, it is important to realize the reality the American education system faces with some of the attrition statistics. In a pre-COVID-19 study, it was determined that teacher attrition is so high, it accounts for close to 90 percent of annual teacher demand. Additionally, that same study found less than one-third of national teacher attrition is the result of retirements.[2] This only emphasizes how COVID-19 exacerbated an already-existing issue.

As a result, school districts are tasked with finding new teachers constantly due to the number of mid-career teachers leaving the profession. National data on teacher attrition rates became available back in 1992 when it was 5.1 percent. Additionally, national data indicate the public-school teacher attrition rate of 7.68 percent in 2012 represented a loss of 238,000 teachers in that year and between 2009 and 2014, teacher education enrollments had a 35 percent reduction.[3]

In 2019, EdWeek reflected on the previous decade to identify the ten most profound ways education has changed in the 2010s.[4] Tougher academic standards, the increasing importance of students' test scores, an influx of new technology and social media, the rise of teen depression and suicide rates, and divisive rhetoric in politics all topped the list, and any educator can speak to these realities on a daily basis. Additionally, continued school shootings and subsequent heart-wrenching trainings, increased duties, responsibilities, and expectations placed on teachers were on the list. As always, teacher pay was also noted, though this one is tricky since teacher pay is hard to argue across the board. Instead, it really depends on what type of school (private, public, charter, online) and where that school is located, so it really is not a universal issue.

It turns out these "glorified babysitters" already felt burned out for a variety of reasons before the global pandemic hit. Regardless, the term has stuck and has only been exacerbated by the rest of the world returning to work in new and innovative ways, like working remotely, all while education remains *remotely* untouched, with typical five-day school weeks where students, teachers, and school administrators come all day every day.

While many people wondered if the pandemic would open a whole new way of doing school virtually and from anywhere, this disruption quickly fell short, as parents everywhere needed alternative locations for their kids so they could go to work for themselves and run errands. This left schools filling the ever-important role of taking care of the nation's kids while also educating them. Work was redefined by many sectors that found themselves determining what purpose they still served and how they could get their employees back to work—whether in person or virtually. One industry remaining the most untouched by changes has been education.

Teachers deserve more credit than they are given for the function they serve in society—that of not only "glorified babysitters" but those who also act as parents, counselors, nurses, and more for everyone else's benefit—all while achieving state standards and delivering curriculum in creative and engaging ways. While the rest of the world's industries shifted in how they deliver their services or do their work, teachers were asked to come back in person and return to "normal" to serve everyone else's children.

It turns out that society decided online school was not the best delivery method for *every* learner, even though it continued to provide a viable new option for many. This is not to say that nobody else had challenges—we all did—rather, this is to say that amid those challenges, educators were asked to adapt and adjust, and to do it quickly, for the sake of the collective children we serve so that others could do the same in their respective industries. Teachers and school administrators were left to come to terms with the necessary and integral role schools serve for society.

In June 2023, We Are Teachers compiled eighteen statistics from notable organizations, such as Education Week, NEA, MDR, and Educators for Excellence, to help shine light on how educators are being overlooked. Some of them include the following:[5]

1. **44** percent of teachers are burned out.

2. **55** percent of educators now indicate that they are ready to leave the profession earlier than planned.

3. **35** percent of teachers say they are likely to quit within the next two years.

4. **80** percent of educators say that taking on more work due to unfilled job openings within their districts is a serious problem.

5. **45** percent of teachers say they do not feel respected by the public.

6. **42** percent of teachers said their teaching suffered because of the state of their mental health.

7. Only **10** percent of educators would strongly recommend the profession to a young adult.

8. **80** percent of school districts reported difficulty hiring new teachers.

9. **65** percent of educators agree the bureaucracy interferes with teaching.

The good news? One of the eighteen facts shared how 66 percent of teachers are still satisfied with their jobs, noting school administration as a pivotal factor. If teachers are still satisfied, how can we capture this and encourage them to persevere while their colleagues leave?

Pay continues to be a reason some teachers leave, with some focusing not only on their paycheck but also on their sanity and time. The media stories can also exacerbate this concept by publishing stories about teachers switching careers to increase income and quality of life instead of focusing on ways to support and lift up teachers in a post-pandemic world. During the pandemic, teaching was viewed as heroic, and teachers were thanked endlessly for adjusting to an online learning model so quickly and going above and beyond to serve the world's children in new and unique ways. A few years later, and in a completely different climate than the pre-pandemic world, teachers now are under intense scrutiny while battling increasing demands, polarization from politics, students with increased behaviors, and continued frustration about pay and respect. Something must give.

Now What?

It is already clear the main story of this decade will be what it is like to teach in a post-COVID-19 world. If all the issues were real in the previous decade, they only stand to be exacerbated by a global pandemic that flipped education on its side. With much of the research focusing mainly on the problems in American schools surrounding teacher attrition, there is little to no conversation or empirical research surrounding teacher retention. Thus, this was the focus of the original study—and this subsequent book—all because there is clearly a gap in the research and surrounding conversation.

What about the teachers who stay in the field? The ones who persevere, who remain consistent for their students over time and demonstrate grit, are the focus of this book. Why are we not celebrating and giving voice to the teachers who show up every day, despite being yelled at, disrespected, physically hurt, or—best-case negative scenario—burned out from the cycle of increasing demands education has put on our frontline workers for students everywhere? There really are teachers who still love the field of education and would choose it again if they had the choice. What about their perspectives?

It is imperative that administrators and school officials capture what it is about the teachers who choose to stay to bring retention to the forefront of the conversation and retain teachers who still want to be there for their students *and* themselves. Moreover, it is important for teachers to feel they have a say in the matter and can learn from one another since there are still thousands of teachers retiring every year, celebrating decades of service to the field.

The Problem

The assumption that teachers must feel engaged and encouraged in their profession to promote longevity and perseverance for the betterment of the field, their students, and the districts that employ them is a helpful narrative that still needs depth and solutions. The rising attrition rate can be attributed to both general teacher burnout as well as systemic, foundational flaws in the American educational system. Regardless, there is a real cost for school districts to address the ongoing teacher attrition annually.[6]

The cost can be twofold. For one, districts expend hundreds of thousands of dollars to recruit, train, and retain teachers. Suburban districts spend around $11,000 to replace and train new teachers. Therefore, even replacing ten teachers in one year within a district—a normal year— would cost the district approximately $110,000 alone, not accounting for inflation.[7]

The other cost of teacher attrition is student achievement and motivation. For example, research has shown that teacher burnout will lead to undermining student motivation.[8] Additionally, it has been found that high turnover rates reduce achievement rates for students whose classrooms are directly affected and for other students in the school.[9]

Teacher attrition is academically and financially costly and negatively predicts student achievement.[10] In addition to the financial cost, there are also costs regarding teacher knowledge about students, the community, and collaborative relationships.[11] Ultimately, a lack of veteran educators can be a detriment to our students because they could be assigned new teachers who lack experience and understanding of the content, field, or best practices, coupled with a lack of the support veteran teachers could provide if they stay.

Leaving the numbers aside and instead focusing on the hearts of teachers who stay, *Washington Post* said it best in an article written in August 2022 titled "There's No Shortage of Teachers. We've Just Driven Them Out of Schools." The article focuses on all the talented teachers out there who are qualified, passionate, and eager…and who also have had enough of the real shortages that are decaying their profession: respect, value, common sense, and safety.[12] In a world where schools are most likely to be blamed for seemingly everything and are the horrific sites of unnecessary tragedy, why would any teacher choose to stay?

There are now entire podcasts, books, businesses, YouTube channels, Facebook groups (with tens of thousands of educators!), and Instagram accounts fully dedicated to sharing about what life after teaching can look like and encouraging educators to utilize the skills they have outside the classroom. Many of these entities are started by former teachers themselves as they share their journey of hitting the threshold and deciding when to leave for their own mental health or for family reasons.

Beyond the world of educators helping educators leave, there are recent books all about quitting, in general, and how it can be the right option for many. In 2022, Annie Duke shared about the power of knowing when to walk away in her book *Quit*.[13] In 2023, Dr. Julia Keller shared about the myth of perseverance and how the new science of giving up can set you free in her book *Quitting*.[14] Both their books share success stories of people from all different walks of life, socioeconomic statuses, and experience levels who found quitting to be their path toward career freedom and better lives.

In a world containing a wealth of information about how teachers can thrive and serve society outside the classroom by leveraging their skills and expertise, and a world that gives them permission to quit by validating this decision, I ask again: Why would any teacher choose to stay?

The Already Known Factors Contributing to Whether Teachers Decide to Stay or Go

The following are factors educators have already used to determine whether they should stay. As a result, they are common themes one may still find in schools now. While these previous and current themes remain important, the next section will uncover the new themes emerging from the study I worked through during fall 2020. The new themes shared later will help elevate the conversation to a discussion more appropriate for a post-COVID-19 educational world. For now, here are the previously researched themes many schools have already adopted.

Mentoring

It is essential for schools to establish a mentoring system to support teachers' growth and retention. Key aspects of an effective mentoring program are that they are well planned, provide opportunities for mutual dialogue, observation, and reflection, all while establishing shared goals.[15] When new teachers receive those types of support, they are less likely to want to leave and more likely to lean into the people who are there to help them. This fosters a community of learning and mentoring that helps keep teachers around and makes them feel like they are truly part of a culture of belonging.

Leadership

Leadership is a major reason—if not the primary one—for teacher attrition.[16] Leadership can be defined in a variety of ways. For example, it can be informal because teachers have proximity to more veteran teachers who take on peer leadership roles. It can also mean having access to the school administrators in the building in which the teacher works. Leadership can also refer to the district office. At the most distant level, teachers can grow weary of leaders at the state or federal levels because of the constant barrage of new mandates they must keep up with year after year.

School leaders who are supportive and accessible are the most effective since there is a magnetic effect, attracting accomplished teachers searching for environments to help them reach their peak performance levels.[17] On the contrary, a lack of administrative support is a key factor in teacher attrition; therefore, it is imperative that administrators in all positions—from district offices to the schools—recognize the responsibility they have in retaining their own staff.

Teacher Preparation Programs

Teacher preparation programs can play a vital role for the futures of their candidates by giving them the necessary social and emotional support that can help give teacher candidates the extra tools they need to succeed. Preservice programs emphasizing the collegial nature of teaching can provide opportunities to forge personal and professional relationships and encourage continuing contact through networks and social events after graduation from college, which all contribute to supporting new teachers as learners and as novices in the field.[18]

Helping early career teachers understand the toll that the profession can take on their own mental and physical well-being is a necessary part of the conversation because of how demanding the career can be, particularly in the first few years. A new teacher's understanding of the reality of teaching is the first step; the second step is connecting them in professional networks—whether through their preparatory university or through their employment district—which can adequately support and grow them as they get started.

Positive School Culture and Climate

Sometimes creating a positive school culture and climate can be as simple as validating teachers for their work and dedication. During the COVID-19 pandemic, this was easy to do. Yet now, after a few years, it has become increasingly difficult for teachers to feel truly valued for not only the work they are doing in the classroom, but also for the services they are providing by taking care of the nation's children while everyone else returns to their respective workplaces, oftentimes in the comfort of their own homes or on a more hybrid or flexible schedule.

Creating an in-house positive school climate promoting high morale can work wonders on a teacher to feel supported, encouraged, and part of something bigger than the struggles they face in their classroom. After all, teachers are the ones who are on the front line—in more ways than one—and treating them with the utmost respect can make a world of difference.[19]

Self-Efficacy

Self-efficacy is considered an important—yet often overlooked—factor because it can be hard to quantify how much self-efficacy a teacher candidate has from an interview process. However, knowing that research suggests a teachers' confidence level is related to their ability to problem-solve and cope with dilemmas that arise makes this determination even more important.[20]

Hiring teachers with high levels of self-efficacy is particularly important because this trait can outweigh positive school climate as a factor in novice teacher success. This is necessary because findings also suggest positive school environments are not enough, in and of themselves, to support struggling teachers. There must be a purposeful, systematic approach and plan to cover teachers with support and guidance.[21]

Resilience

Another factor successful in retaining teachers is hiring new staff who are resilient. This can also be difficult to identify; however, even after hiring, schools should have induction programs offering resilience-building activities and teaching related strategies because early career attrition may be less likely for teachers with strong levels of resilience.[22]

An important job of administrators should be setting new teachers up well so they are not forced to face difficulties in their early years. They should work to provide them with schedules that speak to their strengths, interests, and limited experience while making distinct connections between resilience, teacher development, and retention. Better yet, if districts can appropriately identify strong levels of resilience in their interviewed candidates, then they can lean toward hiring those qualified teachers possessing this important quality.

Teacher resilience is a key to career longevity. New teachers may enhance their resilience by fostering productive relationships with people who understand the trials of teaching, reinforce the value of what teachers do, and offer insight into various options available for dealing with a variety of teaching situations.[23]

This is where a mentoring program comes in: a well-positioned and planned program can provide this type of support. However, if one does exist, it is imperative to be intentional about the veteran teachers who serve as mentors. Jaded veteran teachers in it only for the additional money will not help the cause and could even be counterproductive. Instead, it is important to identify the veteran teachers who have stayed for the right reasons, have demonstrated their own leadership and resilience abilities, and who genuinely yearn to help by building into the new staff members.

Significance in Teacherverance

Teacher attrition was already at an all-time high when certain parts of America with extreme teacher shortages began to aggressively recruit teachers with new incentives. State Departments of Education even began researching alternative routes toward traditional licensure. This was in 2017.[24]

Fast-forward to December 2022, when there was a report on how the pandemic exacerbated a long-standing national shortage of teachers, agreeing the issue in decline had already begun and extending it beyond the pandemic as the decline in teachers continues to exponentially increase.[25]

More long-term implications, unnerving over time, involve how the original study pointed out the slow decline of bachelor's degrees conferred in education, now charting lower than social sciences and history, health professions, and business. As this trend continues while we annually celebrate retirements and bemoan teachers leaving prior to retirement for whatever reasons, this will only continue to intensify the problem.

Additionally, in October 2022, the National Education Association—the largest labor union in the United States, representing public school teachers and other support personnel, including college faculty—published its own study titled "Real Solutions, Not Band-Aids, Will Fix Educator Shortage."[26] This research demonstrates the decline of educators entering the field in a different way—by showing how, between 2009 and 2014, there was a reverse trend of Americans who hoped their kids would enter the education workforce. That trend has only continued to be reversed post-pandemic, as a staggering 62 percent reported they would not want their kids to enter the education field.

It is clear there has been plenty written about this problem; however, most literature focuses on the attrition piece and why so many teachers leave before retirement. On the other hand, there is little focus on the ones who stay—the teachers who choose to endure the more difficult years, see various initiatives come and go, and consistently welcome new staff annually. This is where we will spend the rest of our time.

The *significance* of identifying teacher perseverance traits is to determine whether they can be captured. If so, certain trends can then be gleaned and found important for administrators, college preparation programs, and other decision-makers to replicate to develop a stronger capacity for teacher perseverance. Teacher turnover affects districts regarding costs of both time and money. It takes time to train new teachers, exorbitant staff resources to plan onboarding for new staff, and money to invest in professional development or the completion of early teacher programs attached to licensure.[27] What if, instead, districts could pour more focused and intentional resources into the teachers they must retain and encourage them to stay? This book provides some insight into what may contribute to teacher longevity by identifying factors ripe for helping both district administrators and teacher preparation programs alike across America.

Simply put, students perform better and log fewer absences when instructed by an experienced teacher.[28] Moreover, new teachers perform better when they have more experienced colleagues.[29] Additionally, annually across the United States, about 8 percent of the teacher workforce voluntarily elects to leave the classroom and move onto other career options[30]—and that was before the pandemic. It is now time to do something about it.

Finally, most recently in August 2023, the *Washington Post* reported on the homeschool community growing,[31] thereby offering a larger threat to public education as we know it. With the increasing opportunities through EdChoice or Education Savings Accounts in certain states, families are given countless options for where and how to school their own children, and teachers are given increased flexibility regarding where they can leverage their expertise. Educational technology and micro school companies are thriving, and many are hiring experienced, licensed teachers to help them along the way. Identifying themes of teacher perseverance helps to preserve teaching as we know it— both as a public service to the world's students and to the profession, adding value to their lives daily.

Now that the historical and current context has been revealed, part 2 will share the results of the study upon which this work is based and share the information behind the most relevant identified themes. Then, readers will have the opportunity in part 3 to consider their own stories and to explore questions asking them to think more deeply about their own experiences around education. Part 4 will then look ahead to what can be done, given what we have learned and how we can all move forward with these themes in mind *and* try to make a better future for our educators, which will undoubtedly impact our students.

Part 2

Teacherverance
What Makes
Teachers
Persevere?

Chapter 2
Terms of Teacherverance— The Original Study

The immediate strategies found from this research originally conducted in 2020 surround four themes extracted from the interviews with veteran teachers. With the people in place from every middle and high school in our area, we asked them to complete a Grit Scale survey[32] and participate in individual, semi-structured interviews. Interview transcripts were then analyzed to identify factors that might have contributed to their perseverance. These factors were organized into four themes: a Higher Calling, the Only Option, Community, and Contextual Joy. The term "teacherverance"—and the title of this book—is proposed to capture the essence of this special case of professional longevity to encourage additional research and identify ways to better support classroom teachers over the entire course of their careers.

Fast-forward to 2023: The research seems unexpectedly more pertinent in a post-COVID-19 world of workplace flexibility, independence, and endless choice, with side hustles becoming careers. If school and industry leaders alike could take the time to consider the implications of these four themes on their school, business, or organization, they can help determine ways to engage their employees and retain those who are representing well year after year in new and creative ways that are needed now more than ever.

The four themes identify teaching in the following ways:

- **Higher Calling:** Feeling a sense of awe, spiritual awakening, faith, or otherness as a classroom teacher remains in the field for reasons beyond the classroom, the students, or the school.

- **Community:** Four pathways of how veteran teachers experience community:

  o With their students

  o With their colleagues

  o With the overall community of the district, town, or city

  o With friends or mentors outside of school

- **The Only Option:** This includes a duality of two sides of responses:

  o *Positive/inspiration.* Enthusiasm exudes senses of calm, duty, and purpose, as teachers know they cannot imagine doing any other role, despite its challenges.

  o *Pragmatic/desperation.* Focusing on the necessity of teaching due to the consistent and predictable pay raises, job security, strong insurance, and benefits for their families. This side is where teachers admit the necessary role this job plays and their inability to feel comfortable taking a risk to find something else at the time of frustration.

- **Contextual Joy:** Finding joy in what they do as classroom teachers based on the appropriate contextual factors at the appropriate time in the right environment—school building, having the right leadership team, or enjoying the town or city or students they have taught.

In addition to learning about these themes and their implications, I will share my own story in sections titled "Pers<u>on</u>verance" to personalize the perseverance I have had to tap into throughout my own career. I would not be writing this book if I did not have a personal connection to the topic. The Pers<u>on</u>verance sections are all about how we, as people, can show perseverance—and encourage others to tap into it—by sharing our own personal stories.

To start, the reason for sharing my own story is that it allows you to share yours as you unpack the role you can play and the reasons you stay. Whether you choose to stay for yourself, for your family, or because a great administrator or policymaker removes barriers to allow teachers to *want* to stay, the goal is that you choose teaching rather than feeling obligated, stuck, or desperate.

We all play a role, and you will have a chance to uncover yours in part 3. There you will be prompted to answer the same questions the original veteran teachers answered to help get us here. I encourage you to use that section however you feel best fits. It can be for your eyes only, for you to get a group of teacher friends to connect and share your stories, or for districts to help their teachers uncover their reasons for staying as a way to recognize we are all in this hard—yet important—work together. For now, let's dig into the themes and their implications on my own story; I am confident you will find some connections.

Chapter 3
Higher Calling

Only those with a "true sense of calling" should pursue teaching as a profession.
—Claire Robertson-Kraft & Angela Duckworth, 2014

What has kept me in the field is I have a very driven purpose to fight for the underdogs of society. It is a trait my grandmother has passed onto me. I will not let an "underdog" student be written off. It is their successes that remind me I can do good in the world. I teach [my content] as a side hustle. My purpose for being there is more of a passion for students, youth, and a compassion for who they are.
—Veteran Teacher

"Higher Calling" in teaching is defined as feeling a sense of awe, spiritual awakening, faith, or otherness as a classroom teacher remains in the field for reasons beyond the classroom, the students, or the school. Teachers who mentioned phrases having to do with a higher calling noted their faith in God or some other being, their ability to see the bigger picture, their affirmation that they are working with the right students or staff at the right time, and their interest in getting into teaching in the first place to serve and give back to the community.

Many teachers referenced the generational profession teaching had become and how they wanted to keep the tradition going; teachers discussed their faith in God and an acknowledgment that he had given them a gift to teach and love students well. Additionally, participants mentioned reasons beyond classroom teaching or their content that kept them going, like service to others or focusing on roles they have outside of school that allow them to prioritize what is most important when the situation in school is challenging, allowing them to not be too frustrated with the demands of the job.

Keywords like "calling," "blessed," "blessing," "God," or "faith," along with key terms like "not sweating the small stuff" or "focusing on what really matters, rather than letting the minutiae get to you" were used to identify this trait in veteran teachers. Overall, these words and themes emerged nearly sixty times throughout the interviews.

One veteran teacher mentioned, "As long as I can remember, I wanted to be a teacher. I played teacher in elementary school. I would teach my brothers 'school;' I always felt like it was a calling, even though I had relatives try to talk me out of it. I know this is where I'm supposed to be. I've always felt blessed because I've always known what I want to do."

Another veteran teacher commented along the same lines saying, "I have faith in God; I know God has a plan in my life. He has taken care of me. God put me on this planet to do something. There is someone I'm meant to influence today. That's my job. My dad's whole family is salespeople. I say I am in sales. I sell education."

A third veteran teacher reflected on how they always "try to find relationships with kids, try to find positives everywhere," while admitting they "don't sweat the small stuff." They shared how proud they are because they "can prioritize and focus on the things [they] find important." They know how integral it is to keep calm and have their sanity intact throughout the roller coaster of emotions that comes from challenging school years with increasing demands.

The quote at the beginning of the chapter from a veteran teacher from the study is worth expanding upon:

"What has kept me in the field is I have a very driven purpose to fight for the underdogs of society. It is a trait my grandmother has passed onto me. I will not let an 'underdog' student be written off. It is their successes that remind me I can do good in the world. I teach [my content] as a side hustle. My purpose for being there is more of a passion for students, youth, and a compassion for who they are."

This teacher also shared how they lived in a bubble growing up—attending private schools in the suburbs—and realized they wanted to be part of improving systems to be fairer and more just.

Consequently, this veteran teacher has made it their mission in life by striving to equip students with essential skills of determination, compassion, and passion to help all students succeed. This teacher even noted how "not a lot of people are standing in line to fight for the underdogs, students on [Individualized Education Plans], or the ones just making it day to day. For twenty-three years, I have purposefully taught the [more beginner levels] of [my content]." This higher calling has become their purpose and focus and allows the challenging daily frustrations to not cloud the overall purpose they have set out to achieve by being a classroom teacher.

Teaching as a Higher Calling can show itself in teachers having a faith in a higher power, a sense of service to students, or the belief that they were ultimately called to the profession. Similarly, it can also contribute to the fact that teachers stay despite frustrations or duties they do not like because they know and believe firmly that they are there for bigger and better reasons. They know better than to get caught in the trap of complaining about the small, menial headaches because they are self-assured enough to know that they occur in all workplace environments and they will come and go, while their impact can last for—or shape—entire lifetimes.

***

Pers<u>on</u>verance: How a person can show perseverance through sharing their own personal story.

Pers<u>on</u>verance trait: Higher Calling—Feeling a sense of awe, spiritual awakening, faith, or otherness as a classroom teacher remains in the field for reasons beyond the classroom, the students, or the school.

I have always felt a particular transcendence toward education. My faith has been a huge part of my career journey because I feel led every step of the way—from finding the right context that brings me the most joy to giving me other opportunities that have helped me clarify my own "only option" and sense of community, and I am forever grateful.

The higher calling for me was—through the ups and downs—knowing God had it in control the whole time and feeling a sense of calm throughout the most challenging years. That when I was confused, frustrated by the "system," or let down by any other external factors, I could always count on knowing my faith would lead me steady and still sure of the path I was on. My faith first became personal to me when I was in high school and has been solidified throughout my professional career since then.

The first moment this was tested was my first experience being on the receiving end of a reduction in force. When my principal at the time told me in the spring there would be no position at the same school next year, I was equally devastated and calm. The devastated part was simply because I am a human who loved the first school community that I landed in. The calm part ultimately won over due to an immediate reminder of how strongly I felt grounded in my faith and the journey a God I had come to know and love had in store for me.

This has been what has kept me going through the tumultuous years, with many frustrating moments leading me to focus on the many more positive and encouraging ones. Through six buildings and five districts in the first ten years of my professional career, I was steadfast in the belief that each change brought about the best in me and gave me exactly what I needed, even if I did not necessarily like it. This was faith in motion tested with each transition.

Regardless of a person's faith belief system, anyone who submits to a higher sense of self is better equipped to handle the challenges coming from the daily workplace environment. It is important that in the highs and lows of any role, each person can maintain a steadiness untouched by the turbulence. For teachers, this is even more important when pay, demanding schedules, challenging student (or their family) behaviors, and feelings of being underappreciated or overlooked all can take a toll if left unchecked by a Higher Calling.

Chapter 4
Community

I can't imagine going anywhere else. Truly. I really enjoy the people I work with. I feel a part of the community—I've been there forever. I feel a part of it. I've seen families go through, siblings, etcetera. I have a history and reputation.
—Veteran Teacher

There are four ways the theme of community emerged in the interviews: one is regarding the community created in a classroom with the students, the second is the community created within a school building among colleagues who become like family, and the third is the way the community as a whole district, town, or city can contribute to longevity. Finally, outside of the school community is the community a teacher creates or already has by way of mentors, family members, and friends who keep teachers going emotionally. Therefore, teaching as Community has four pathways: (1) students; (2) colleagues (administrators and teachers); (3) the overall community of the district, town, or city; and (4) the community found outside of school with friends or mentors.

Community in the Classroom with Students

Veteran teachers continually expressed the importance of how everything they do—even all the extras—goes back to the students, confirming they are the central reason they stay. Many teachers expressed how the students—not only in their current class but also those whom they have had that come back to give their thanks—leave an impact on them.

When asked why they stayed, nearly half of those interviewed specifically mentioned students as at least one of the reasons.

One veteran teacher was describing their personality as a teacher and then went into how those attributes can permeate into their work with the students:

"Caring, nurturing, loving people, I think, comes across first in the classroom—it's about how you care for the students. More than anything—that's what's happening! I like math, and I do want to make sure my kids come out of that classroom with a knowledge of math. But more than anything, I just want them to know they're cared for."

If teachers stay in the profession long enough, sometimes they can see former students join the ranks as colleagues who teach in the same building or even, in some cases, become administrators. This can help perpetuate the sense of belonging they feel in the chosen school community and reinforce the work they do by showing how it works and creates successful students to set them up for a positive future as well. One teacher was proud to share their experience in this way:

"We all have those moments—those aha moments when you get the opportunity to share that joy of recognition. 'I know this!' [on a student's face] is a magical experience. It keeps you going! I have more fun now than I did thirty years ago. I might be the most veteran person in the building. I have had the opportunity to be led by former students. I get to see people every day that I knew when they were younger. If you're enthusiastic, teaching helps keep you young. I am the youngest person in the room, at least in my heart. Those of us who choose to stay—that's the reason why."

With the focus on students, it was easy for teachers to continue sharing not only how they persevered because of—not despite—the students but also advice for younger teachers, like one teacher who shared this: "Young teachers—teach kids first, then teach them curriculum. Do it in that order! Lots of teachers make the mistake of focusing on their curriculum." This is a good time to remind readers this study was done with secondary teachers only. Oftentimes elementary teachers are known for teaching students, while secondary teachers can be known for teaching their content. It is an important reminder for all teachers and school administrators that content or test scores should *never* be prioritized over students.

Another veteran teacher who commented on their passion for students, focused on helping students find their own passion: "I genuinely love what I do. I love seeing the kids do well, what happens after they leave and come back. I've had kids invite me to their weddings and thank me for what I did." This teacher then goes on to share, on behalf of the students, how "kids need good teachers more than they have ever needed them. They need human interaction more than ever because they are getting less of it." There can be an argument made for how increasing negative student behaviors, coupled with feeling like there is a lack of support from school administration or families, are reasons teachers are leaving. However, this teacher realizes how, with phones and technology, "There is going to come a moment when people are going to realize what has happened. Human interaction matters most. I do what I do because I love the feeling of helping them, the feeling of: 'Thank you; you helped me find a passion.'"

Finally, one teacher reinforces the idea of focusing on students over content as well as the long-term impacts a teacher can have by proudly saying:

"More days happen when I have something that has filled my heart and made me happy and know where I am is right. Students are what make me stay. Yes, I teach [my content], but that's not my driving force; it's teaching kids. The best thing you can give a student is the confidence to do whatever they're going to do. If they have confidence, everything is going to fall into place. I have former students who become adults and are being successful that I keep in touch with, who struggled when they were younger, and they are making it work now. I love still having contact with them".

Community in the School with Colleagues

Veteran teachers also continually expressed the importance of building strong relationships with other teachers, administrators, and staff members within the building. Many of these teachers used the word "family" when describing these relationships and noted how administrators and colleagues have gotten them through difficult times in their careers. Again, almost half specifically mentioned these collegial relationships as some of the reasons that keep them going.

One teacher spoke on this theme enthusiastically: "You need your tribe. If I didn't have amazing colleagues, I don't know if I would have lasted. Luckily, we all fall apart on different days. We really support one another in this building. You need to have your people!"

"Family" does not have to be the only way to describe teaching. It can be a failed metaphor in many contexts since workplace families have to operate differently than families at home. Because many teachers find a district and stay, due to pay scales and a lack of movement in the field in general, it is more common for teachers to stay these days and do life together than most other professions, which have become increasingly more transient. Additionally, teachers and school administrators know their friends and family—no matter how well-intentioned they are—truly have no concept of what a typical school day looks like, which deepens the importance of leveraging the relationships and shared experiences inside the school. Therefore, colleagues really do remain for a full career and offer the necessary support that oftentimes cannot be found outside of school.

Community in the District, City, or Town

This one lends itself to the next point—teaching as Contextual Joy. There will be more to come on that one soon. This study was completed with current public school teachers who commented on the importance of entire communities coming together, though some also had previous private school experience. Either way, many participants emphasized how the support of the town, city, or district they serve can have a lasting impact on their overall happiness and job satisfaction. While there may be many factors as to why someone would not move into a school district in which they work, many veteran teachers note how they found a sense of community in their districts, which helped them feel like they belonged and were more invested in the work they were doing and the community they were helping.

One teacher gave advice to a new teacher, stating plainly, "Move into the district. I live across the street. Commit yourself to the community. I don't have a commute, which is one of the reasons I'm still here! Knowing the kids from my neighborhood, seeing the places they work. It's not imperative; it helps to be committed and establish yourself."

The shadow side of this one worth mentioning—though beyond the scope of this book to explore—comes from the book *Savage Inequalities,* originally written in 1991 and republished since with some updates, by Jonathan Kozol. This book shares the alarming disparities existing between schools that are miles away from one another in various cities due to racial or socioeconomic issues.[33] The reality is there are students who deserve the best education *everywhere,* and the current educational infrastructure is not set up well to support them *or* the teachers serving them. This makes it hard to stay when teachers and school administrators have their own families at home to support. Communities of districts and towns still need and rely on competent and dedicated teachers who see value in staying.

Community as Mentors, Family, and Friends

Particularly evident in the question about how they got into teaching, many veteran teachers recounted the people (relatives, former teachers, or friends) who helped inspire their own educational and professional journey. It was made clear that perseverant teachers relied on their own network outside of school to help support them emotionally and mentally throughout their career. One teacher shared: "When I was first teaching, I was the youngest teacher in the team. A big part of my longevity was being with those mentors who taught me. I had the gut instinct, but they taught me all the things you just don't have naturally. They were kind and patient, and I'm still good friends with them to this day."

Regardless of the *type* of community noted, it is clear how impactful teachers feeling part of a larger community is and how it can keep them going when demands are high and appreciation is low. Connecting teachers with the community in a variety of ways can help them feel a sense of belonging and give them resources to recognize the reach they have. Teaching alone in a classroom can feel isolating; being connected to a student alumni community, the district, the town, or close colleagues all can help transform the isolating feeling into connectedness.

***

Personverance: How a person can show perseverance through sharing their own personal story.

Personverance trait: Community—feeling connected to the people or the area in which one teaches.

At the time of writing this, I have been in education as a profession for just shy of fifteen years. In that amount of time, I have had the unique experience of being part of six school communities in five different districts; consequently, I have learned a lot about the impact any community has on the environment for teachers and school administrators alike. It is important to mention how all districts face similar challenges and have similar stakeholders in their systems, even if they play out differently. The strength of a surrounding school or district community can truly make or break an educator's experience, and this has been witnessed increasingly more as political lines have been drawn and needs of students have increased in a post-COVID-19 world.

Person_on_verance: Community in the Classroom with Students

I had the distinct pleasure of landing a full-time job right out of college at the school where I also did my student teaching placement. Therefore, I already knew some of the students and even immediately got involved in a mentorship nonprofit in the area, which included traveling out of state with students I would be teaching the following year. Since I was fresh out of college and teaching high school students, I was only a few years older than these students. We quickly connected through the summer trip, and then as the school year progressed, I got to know them better. In fact, I ended up teaching full time, coaching every season I taught (volleyball in the fall, basketball in the winter, lacrosse in the spring), *and* continuing the mentorship nonprofit work. Therefore, some students saw me during the day as their teacher, after school at sports practice as their coach, and then later in the evening at events as their mentor.

This season of my professional life provided the opportunity to make strong connections with the community of students I was serving. Plus, the reality of how close we were in age meant that as soon as they graduated high school and went to college, we ended up becoming friends and keeping in touch. Many of them even went on to become teachers! I have since traveled domestically and internationally with some of these former students—places like Seattle, New York, Norway, New Zealand, Spain, Sweden, Finland, and even Estonia—all because of the connections we made when they were in high school and I was in my early-to-late twenties, spending school days, afternoons, and evenings with the students I was fortunate enough to serve. They were my community, and working with them in these various contexts was a deeply meaningful way to begin a teaching career.

Personverance: Community in the School with Colleagues

I have had incredible colleagues throughout my career. Thankfully, the tough years have never been marked by challenging colleagues or administrators. I have always felt part of a larger team who cares about me, each other, the school, the work, and of course, the students. Consequently, I recognize the power of being sent a fun surprise through interoffice mail, getting an encouraging text in the evening, doing a shared workout before or after school (because nobody else has the same type of schedule!), having people who will listen to you through tears and still trust you are the right person for the job, laughing (sometimes through tears too!) about the moments of the day only your hallway friends will understand, or being able to share an admirable success story with other teachers who can truly appreciate it.

Colleagues in all environments can offer a strong support system; in teaching, however, they can truly make or break the career experience since so much of a teacher's time is spent with students. It is important for them to know that when they leave their classroom bubbles, they are still well supported by their administrators, custodians, administrative assistants, and fellow teachers.

Pers<u>on</u>verance: Community in the District, City, or Town

As mentioned, I have been part of five school districts in five different cities for me to have accurately tested this one. One district I was in for a short amount of time, and even then, I could tell its small size (fewer than two thousand students in grades K through 12) helped the teachers who had been there forever feel intimately connected to the families, students, and the shared stories they would tell.

Personally, I grew up in—and attended—the same school district where my mom went, which was larger (fewer than six thousand students in grades K through 12). When I was given a chance to return there to teach (the same year my mom was set to retire), it was an obvious choice. Teaching in the same junior high where my mom and I both attended was a dream come true. To take the dream one step further, when I had graduated from high school, the senior superlative votes came in, and I was voted "Most Likely to Teach" in the same district. So really, I was helping at least one senior superlative—the dream backed by the votes of my classmates—come true.

This experience cemented the importance of community as an educator because it finally provided me the chance to proudly become a second-generation teacher and student and was my first taste at serving the community where I was raised and then lived in as an adult. I rode my bike to and from school, alongside teachers and students in the same building, coached and taught students in my own community, and got to "do life" with the colleagues I had—all because of our shared proximity for work and play. I even had the chance to teach students who were kids of my mom's students. What a joy!

Teacherverance

• •

After three years of the homebound experience and fulfilling all my childhood and classmates' dreams, I unexpectedly found myself taking a job across the river in another state. I knew this came with an undesirable longer commute time and instead found an apartment immediately across the street from the school, giving me the chance to walk from one side of the crosswalk to the other (yes, with the same students I was teaching) daily on my four-minute walking commute from inside my apartment to inside my classroom.

A quaint, walking community (just over three thousand students total in grades K through 12) with a lunch break where students could walk home and no school-provided transportation—this school experience gave me another glimpse into the benefits of living and teaching in the same community. It particularly helps when the community is supportive of its teachers and takes pride in the education the school offers its students, like this one did.

The kind of community that has a local coffee shop down the street from the school that changes hours and plans based on the school's schedule. The kind of community that has a church across the street providing free meals to the students who choose to join them for daily off-campus lunches. The kind of community that comes together for Friday night lights for generations, not just the current students and families. There is strength in this kind of community, and if teachers are lucky enough to find something like that, they seldom leave.

The only reason I left is because I had the opportunity to go from teaching to school administration. "Community of a district, city, or town" took on another persona as I saw it through a new lens. Regardless, the two communities I have served as a school administrator have been large (around ten thousand students total in grades K through 12) and therefore have a much larger reach regarding resources, community partnerships, and opportunities. Tapping into those resources from the administrator side to support teachers can lead to teachers feeling more connected, because otherwise, the large size of a district or school can be overwhelming. I am grateful to have been in various environments that have all given me a sense of community and pride.

Pers_onverance: Community as Mentorship, Family, and Friends

There is nothing like teaching alongside your heroes— whether they are mentors, family, or friends. Feeling a sense of community with your colleagues is one thing; compounding that feeling with a stronger, more intimate connection of people who know you deeply is on another level. Naturally, I have felt this more at some places than others, yet all six schools I have found myself in have given me at least one mentor or person I can call a friend.

I mentioned earlier how special it was to have spent my first year teaching at the school I attended, which was also the final year of my mom's entire teaching career. What a full-circle moment! Sharing this with her is something I will never forget, and it truly felt like a proverbial passing of the torch. With pride, I continued her and my dad's legacies as dedicated professional educators. Additionally, in this same school, there were still teachers who taught me when I attended that school as a student. They were the reasons, beyond my family, for why I went into education, and there I was, eating lunch with them in the "staffeteria" while recounting stories of our days in our current collegial relationship and our past in our previous teacher/student relationship.

Then, in my most challenging years, after multiple times being on the receiving end of tough reduction-in-force decisions, admired mentors and administrators of mine encouraged me to not give up hope and instead practice resilience. They gave me the story I needed to remind me of how my teaching was not yet over. They wrote the recommendation letters for me, helped me decide on a college for a doctoral program and administrative licensure, and sent me on my way, equipped with the belief that the best was still to come. This helped take my mind off the challenging days and gave me a reason to stay. "Community through mentors, family and friends"—their belief in me and my leadership abilities—was truly what kept me going, which is also the reason you are reading this now.

Chapter 5
The Only Option

There are two ways this theme of "the Only Option" came to life in the interviews: one is more positive or idealistic, and the other is more pragmatic or realistic.

Positive/Inspiration

I couldn't imagine what else I would do that I would enjoy as much as I do now. It's a good living. I can't imagine anything else. I would stay because I love it. I don't dread going to work.
—Veteran Teacher

When teachers discussed classroom teaching as the only option as a positive, they used phrases indicating they could not imagine life any other way, stressing the importance of classroom teaching for the sake of being on the front lines with the students, or choosing to look at the positives of the roles and not letting the negatives affect their wanting to leave completely.

These teachers were enthusiastic, passionate, self-proclaimed lifelong learners, and focused on doing what was best for their students and for themselves. In the interview, when asked about who they are as people, these teachers spoke of the commitment they made when they got into the profession and focused on how they genuinely like their roles and feel a sense of duty and obligation to their students and colleagues to stay. The positive side is the idea of teachers not being able to picture doing anything else because of how much they ultimately love the role, despite its challenges.

Teacherverance

Some keywords and phrases for the positive side of this theme were "always," "all," and only," like one teacher who noted, "All I ever wanted to do was be a teacher. Mom is a teacher; my aunt is a teacher. It's in our family. I've always loved school!" This teacher was not alone, as many teachers were part of a family of teachers or felt a sense of purpose toward teaching from loving to "play" school when they were kids, so it was always the top choice as a profession.

Pragmatic/Desperation

Teaching is one of the only professions where, once you pass a certain number of years, the money is good, and you can't do anything else. That money does become a factor in making decisions. When you're closer to retirement, it makes a big difference. It will affect your retirement for the rest of your life. It makes it hard to try somewhere new.
—Veteran Teacher

When teachers discussed classroom teaching as their only option as pragmatic, they used phrases surrounding the necessity of teaching. With few exceptions, teachers tend to receive consistent pay raises over the years, have job security, and can secure good insurance and benefits for their families. Additionally, some teachers noted they did not want to start over elsewhere, go back to school, or figure out how to use their education degrees in other careers. The desperate side is the idea that teachers cannot leave due to the bills it pays or the healthcare it provides to their families.

Twelve teachers particularly noted health insurance, pay, or the need to keep a job when asked for the reasons they stayed. While these teachers never explicitly expressed feeling stuck, they did wonder—with few ideas—what else they could do outside of teaching. They lamented there were not many other options past the fifteen-year mark in their careers. For example, one teacher mentioned actively trying to go into administration for the last three years with no success. They then admitted:

"What's kept me in the classroom is that I just can't land an administration job. I get passed over. What's keeping me in the classroom is, honestly, I need my paycheck. With what can seem like few leadership opportunities available for teachers, it can add to some teachers feeling stuck in a position they do not actually want as classroom teaching increasingly becomes more challenging."

Overall, most teachers were still immensely grateful for the lifestyle teaching can provide.

Whether teachers are inspired to teach—seeing it as "the Only Option" in a positive way—or feeling desperate to keep teaching out of fulfilling a practical need, it is important to uncover the reasons for staying to ensure there is a clear throughline for *why* they are continuing to serve students as teachers. This helps when times are tough and keeps teachers grounded to their "Only Option" for staying.

***

Pers_on_verance: How a person can show perseverance through sharing their own personal story.

Pers_on_verance trait: The Only Option—feeling either pulled to inspiration and positivity regarding why one stays in education *or* feeling desperate and more pragmatic about staying.

I started this book sharing about winter break of the 2014–15 school year—my fourth full school year teaching—and I was already researching ways out of the profession. This was part of my professional journey many do not know. However, if part of uncovering our purpose in persevering through the hard moments is being vulnerable and sharing with others what is truly keeping us going, it is necessary for me to share here in hopes it inspires or gets you—or others—to a new space of sharing as well.

So it is winter break 2014; I want to resign and not come back in January. The expectant teacher who excitedly entered the teaching force fewer than five years ago has lost all hope after having experienced a reduction in force (teachers losing their jobs solely based on years of experience, due to annual enrollment or class number fluctuation) *twice*. Teaching was always "the Only Option" in a positive and inspirational way until those moments. However, I felt frustrated early on, as I learned how circumstances completely out of my control, despite my commitment to the district and school, would lead to unexpected job changes.

Thankfully, I had some great mentors and parents who helped me latch onto a new story for what my "Only Option" would be. They pointed me in a new direction and encouraged me to enroll in a dual doctoral and administrative licensure program at the local university. These trusted mentors, friends, and family members knew I did not actually *want* to resign; circumstances had me stuck, feeling like I would never be able to find myself teaching in the right *context* or *community* again. So I subscribed to "the Only Option" rule by telling myself I could *not* resign and find something new *until* I graduated from my doctoral program. This goal provided a new sense of purpose and identity, separate from the frustrations I was finding in the day-to-day, which served me well for the next five-and-a-half years. During that time, I ended up working in four roles in four districts, and while it was certainly a whirlwind, it gave me a whole new network of educators and renewed resolve to stay in education because of these experiences.

Making teaching the Only Option for myself for these five-and-a-half years was different than feeling like it was the Only Option when I graduated college because I knew more about who I was as an educator, who I wanted to be, and how I wanted to be on the positive side of change. I want to be very clear here: I can say with full confidence that with every step of my journey, I was surrounded by *amazing* teachers, students, and administrators. It was never the people; it was always the circumstances or bureaucracy that led me to be frustrated and burned out early on.

Sometimes anyone of any employment level can be skilled in something or surrounded by kind, well-intentioned people without feeling the true sense of purpose or fulfillment they seek. This was me, and I was determined to find something different by transferring the desperate, pragmatic energy back into one that was positive and inspirational. Thankfully, those varied experiences in such a short amount of time helped me get there by giving myself a new story of what the Only Option meant for me.

Chapter 6
Contextual Joy

[I] need change, diversity, variety. Need to always be learning. I am one of those people that, if I feel like I'm in a rut, I get frustrated, unhappy. I look at people who have been with this district and I wonder, "How have you never gone anywhere else for thirty years?" Bouncing around has really been what keeps me moving. When it wasn't stimulating intellectually, I knew something would change. Oftentimes it was beyond my control, but it ended up being just what I needed.
—Veteran Teacher

For the most part, the context kept me in. [My district] is very supportive and particularly the teaming aspect of it. I thought it was the greatest thing ever. Workload. Fewer classes when I started. Plan time and team time were built in. That was the context that made me excited to come to work that day.
—Veteran Teacher

Sometimes it is not *teaching* that is the issue or makes the work challenging; instead, the *context* can be an important factor in finding the work meaningful or sustainable. It was clear in the interviews that the participating veteran teachers found *joy* in what they do as classroom teachers. It was made apparent that joy is not fixed; instead, veteran teachers noted how their joy could be influenced by their various environments—school buildings, content areas, administrators they have worked with, towns or cities they have served in, or students they have taught. While the participants had at least fifteen consecutive years of classroom teaching experience, not all that experience was in the same environment.

Some had taught online before going into the classroom, some had switched states, and some had switched districts within the same city. Therefore, a common theme noted was the joy that came from finding the right context that worked for them. One veteran teacher admitted, "I have wondered if I had stayed in [state they were in], if I would have stayed in that district or in that profession."

Another teacher focused on the right context by giving the advice to young teachers: "I wouldn't stop and just be satisfied you have a job. Really look for the fit—staff, building, district, students. Find it as early as you can in your career." This is a challenging reality in the world of education— experience does not hold the same weight as it does in other industries. It is important to point out that the teacher commented on finding it as *early* as one can in their career because many districts cannot hire teachers with experience due to experience-based pay scales and teachers becoming too expensive past a certain point.

Many other industries seek out employees with decades of experience, looking for people who are talented with a depth and breadth of knowledge; education, on the other hand, has always had to look at experience as a deterrent due to the years of experience bringing in a higher pay scale and benefits package for that teacher. Consequently, teachers who understand this nuance are often left working hard to find the right fit as quickly as possible and then staying the remainder of their careers to continue up the pay scale, for better or for worse.

There are a variety of contexts teachers can find joy in, whether it is content, grade level, community, or location. One teacher focused on their interest in finding the proper grade level: "I wouldn't want to go below [a certain grade level]. I don't think I would enjoy the conversations with students as much and be able to push their thinking." The implication for school administrators is that if there is a teacher who might be struggling to thrive, they should help them—and the students they serve and the colleagues they work with—by having open and honest conversations about them finding their fit regarding grade level and content area.

Finally, Contextual Joy can present itself to keep teachers going, if the environment is positive, friendly, inviting, and motivating. On the other hand, the context can be debilitating for a career and ultimately be the reason a teacher chooses to leave. All of these demonstrate the multiple layers that emerge in the narratives of the veteran teachers and can act as motivators for new teachers who quickly find themselves burned out within the first few years and considering other career opportunities. Instead, it could be a matter of their administrators or colleagues in other contexts to help them uncover which context would best bring them joy.

***

Personverance: How a person can show perseverance through sharing their own personal story.

Personverance trait: Contextual Joy—the job title of "classroom teacher" is not what brings joy; instead, it is the context in which one teaches, whether that be content area, grade level, community, or colleagues.

As I mentioned earlier, within the first eleven years of my educational career, I found myself in six schools in five different districts across two states, covering six grade levels and four job titles. In the Community section, I commented on how this helped me understand how much community matters. Suffice it to say, I also learned quickly the importance of *context*. I saw how the same players existed in every school—from the motivated young teachers eager to change the world, coach all the sports, and lead all the activities to the veteran teachers who had seen it all, including the cycles of "new" educational jargon or strategies that unsurprisingly seem like what they learned about in their teacher preparation classes decades ago to everything in between.

In educator Ron Clark's book *Move Your Bus: An Extraordinary New Approach to Accelerating Success in Work and Life,* he uses the bus metaphor to describe the various types of people we tend to see in all workplace environments, including schools.[34] If the organization is the bus, there are people in it that can help or hinder a team's ability to move forward:

Drivers who propel and steer the organization.

Runners who go above and beyond to move the mission of the organization forward.

Joggers who do their own jobs without pushing themselves or others.

Walkers who are simply getting pulled along.

Riders who hinder success and can drag the entire team or organization down.

A strong leader can recognize and identify which of their members fall into each category by encouraging them to keep the overall bus moving by working together, even within their various abilities. A strong leader can also recognize when the context is not working for someone and identify ways to get them into a better context. In the case of schools, this is of the utmost importance now, due to fewer teachers coming out of teacher preparation programs. School leadership needs to be equipped to help teachers find their right context to help retain them *and* help serve the students.

Additionally, it is important for new teachers to recognize that just because their first few years of teaching might be challenging and they might consider leaving the profession altogether, they could first consider a new context. They might be able to identify their own roles in the school and determine that if they are a Rider, Walker, or even Jogger, it might be time to consider another context to achieve Runner status. Maybe it is the grade level or the school district, colleagues, or the content area that leads them to be dissatisfied.

Some teachers prefer private schools, while others prefer public or independent or charter schools. Some high school teachers prefer teaching advanced juniors or seniors, while others prefer teaching beginner classes for freshmen and sophomores. Some early and middle-level teachers are certified in two content areas and find one more fulfilling than the other. Of course, leadership, unions, and community support can all play roles in how satisfied a teacher is with their career. Again, it is all about the context.

For me, I knew certain contexts were better than others, even when people would encourage me by saying, "You're so good at this" or "The students love you." While these intentions were kind and not entirely overlooked, I knew in my heart how I felt each day, and if I became consistently emotional over small things, I also knew that particular context was not right for me. Instead of quitting completely, I was able to lean into mentors and outside professional opportunities by adding to my network and to my certifications and qualifications to get me into additional contexts. All of this helped me eventually find immense joy and satisfaction in my career—something I truly want for everyone, especially if it helps talented teachers stay and students succeed.

Part 3

Reflection

What About
My Own
Teacherverance?

Chapter 7
Teacher Interview Questions

Since we now have considered the four themes—Higher Calling, Community, the Only Option, and Contextual Joy—emerging from these interviews and conversations from the veteran teachers, we will look at the seven questions leading to these themes and examine veteran teacher responses. Teachers with any experience are encouraged to take the time and pause to consider their own responses to each question. Additionally, school administrators are encouraged to consider not only their own responses of how they would have answered when teaching but also to take it one step further, to examine the implications of teacher responses with the work being done to support their own staff.

Consider doing this in a school community, in a department, or even for professional development. If you happen to be reading this and are *not* in education, I hope there are universal workplace truths in the questions that can still help you and that this book gives you ideas of how to better support the teachers in your life.

Question 1

Q1: Why did you become a teacher?

In responding to this opening question, the majority of participants referenced people—either family members or former teachers—who helped them see their potential as classroom teachers.

Most participants mentioned a mentor, teacher, or family member who ultimately helped inspire them to begin teaching. George Couros, an author, speaker, and educator, compiled a book called *Because of a Teacher* that speaks to this concept, in which current educators share their personal, heartfelt, and uplifting stories to paint a picture of what impacts the *people* in education had on them.[35]

"There were also some who pointed out the skills for—or the love of—the content they experienced and how they wanted to use them to create a career. Speaking to both these points, one veteran teacher mentioned:

"I was one of the few people that always knew what I wanted to do. I loved communicating with people, writing, and instructing. We do have a strong educational background in my family. I really love serving others; I've always felt that need, and it's my way of being happy with myself. Teaching and a love of [content]—there is a need, and I wanted to serve others."

While not every answer fell into one of these four themes, there was a clear sense of duty and obligation to serving others or honoring their family that emerged. No one person mentioned pay being a factor, and surprisingly, only two of the over forty talked about having the summers off.

Q1: A Higher Calling

"I don't think there's a more important profession on the planet. Not everybody could have an education. I'm here to help you see what you like and don't like. I love teaching. I think it's the most important profession in the world."

"I wanted to do something that made the world a better place to be. [My high school] motto was 'to become a man for others.' I embraced that."

Q1: The Only Option

"I was always destined to be a teacher. It was the only thing that ever appealed to me."

Q1: Community

"I always have a heart to help and serve. Didn't necessarily know teaching was the route I wanted to take. When I went to [college], I met with an advisor, and I was undecided. Knew I was interested in the deaf population. Thought that might be a route I wanted to take. Once I met with him and he had me take Introduction to Special Education, he immediately thought that was the route. Second quarter, he had me take another class. By spring quarter of my freshman year, I eventually said, 'Maybe you're right; I might be interested in special education,' and then he laid out my plan because I liked helping and serving them. Growing up, I was from a small, rural community. Special education did not look like it did [where I am now], even in the eighties. Didn't see any inclusion. It was more for multi-handicapped. I learned what it actually is and was interested. That immediately became my path."

Q1: Contextual Joy

"Started out in microbiology and wanted to do research. Junior year, I realized I loved science, but I didn't want to be stuck in a lab, working in isolation. I wanted to be with people.

I thought, 'I can't live like this!' I didn't want to disappoint my parents. Didn't want to go to school longer…started looking at options and always enjoyed teaching and working with others, so I met with my advisor and secondary science ed was doable, and I could end with just an extra semester."

Pers<u>on</u>verance

What about you? Why did you become a teacher? With which theme does your answer most resonate—Higher Calling, Community, the Only Option, or Contextual Joy? And if you've moved from teaching into something similar, like coaching, administration, etcetera, what helped you make that move? What have you missed or enjoyed about the transition? Encouragement: Share your answer with others.

Question 2

Q2: As you look back on your career, have you had any experiences that even momentarily made you rethink your decision to become a teacher or to consider *leaving* the education profession? If so, why did you decide to *stay* as a classroom teacher, despite that situation?

For Q2, teachers discussed not even "letting their minds go there" and never considered leaving as an option. They also showed signs of optimism, believing that the situation would get better (Higher Calling), the ineffective administrator would leave, the class of students would be better next year, or they would get a different job teaching a different content or in a different school (Contextual Joy). Seven teachers even quickly said they had not even reconsidered quitting or thought about other opportunities at all.

Even more simple than a Higher Calling, one teacher put their focus plainly when discussing all the frustrations that can come with administrative tasks unrelated to the actual teaching: "My mission is to teach my classroom."

Q2: A Higher Calling

"It wasn't about education—I had to stop myself and ask—I'm here to serve. Do I have the ability to educate the whole child and to last at least thirty years? It was more about digging…I do have a strong faith. God kept me going."

Q2: The Only Option

Positive/Inspiration: "I never did think about quitting, even though my starting job was at [a challenging school]."

Pragmatic/Desperation: "I stayed because of the money and had kids to put through college."

Q2: Community

"Yes, there have been some frustrations with big changes in parent support. That is very overwhelming to deal with day to day. The biggest thing that has kept me in it is that I know this is what I want to do, and you have so many benefits that outweigh those bad moments. Coworkers are best friends, and administration is supportive."

Q2: Contextual Joy

"Things that happened to me in my first three years I have never had happen since. I was stressed out a lot. I got out of that. It seems like a river you're in when I was going down the rapids. I just figured I would get out of the rapids at some point."

"I also stayed by switching different positions of teaching to refresh myself."

Pers<u>o</u>nverance

What about you? Have you ever—even momentarily—considered leaving the education field? Do you know people who have? What has their experience been and what has kept you going? With which theme does your answer most resonate—Higher Calling, Community, **the** Only Option, or Contextual Joy? Encouragement: Share your answer with others.

Question 3

Q3: Have you ever considered taking on another role *in* **the education profession? If so, discuss your decision to stay as a classroom teacher.**

The purpose of this question was to gauge how many participants had considered leaving the field of education completely compared to remaining in the field but leaving classroom teaching. Common options for classroom teachers, if they are exploring something different within education, are school counselor, administrator, supervisor, curriculum director, instructional coach, or instructional technology integration specialist. Even though these roles are still within the scope of the industry, the intent was to explore why teachers considered leaving in order to focus on their *teacherverance* as they chose to stay, despite continuing to hold a possibly challenging position.

Nearly half of the participants had never considered it. One answer was incredibly definitive: "Nope! I have no desire to be an administrator, counselor, etcetera. I like having my own classroom with my own students." On the other hand, there were a few vulnerable enough to share they had not only considered but had also even applied to various positions and had not yet been hired. One teacher shared they were "actively trying to go into administration for the last three years. Finished second master's in administration— what's kept me in the classroom is that I just can't land an administrative job. I get passed over."

Finally, more than half expressed having considered something different within education while ultimately deciding to stay in the classroom. Many had their licenses in something else simply for the pay increase or learning, while never intending to use that additional licensure. One teacher even shared they were working on their administrative license, which was the process that helped them understand more clearly it was *not* what they wanted to do.

Beyond the "yes" or "no," this question sought to understand whether teachers had considered leaving classroom teaching at all and, if so, what kept them in the classroom. While many expressed either interest in or were approached about other positions, three admitted to trying to leave classroom teaching and not getting the jobs they applied for. Ultimately, all four themes were covered in various ways as teachers shared their stories of considering leaving their own classroom teacher roles.

Q3: A Higher Calling

"Anytime I'm asked where I see myself in five years, it's always the classroom. I don't want to see all the [challenging parts], discipline, etcetera. I prefer to work on the positive. I try to praise the good behavior and watch them change. I'm at school at 7:10 a.m. and sometimes stay until 5:00 or 6:00 p.m....there are nights where I'm at my table until **eleven** o'clock at night…I work on Saturdays and Sundays…I have thirty-one years in and should be able to just say, 'I've done it before,' but it's a different batch of kids, so it's always different. It's really my passion."

Q3: The Only Option

"I was working on my administrative license and came to a point where I enjoyed teaching ultimately—that's what I wanted to do. Didn't even finish the license because I knew it's not what I wanted. During the coursework, I decided I want to teach."

Q3: Community

"I've been blessed to work with a few very good administrators in a few years. I think the work they do is important but it's not what I want to do. I have a passion for the student council, the students, and the community work we do...if there were a teaching role that would engage me more in the community outreach, I would do it in a heartbeat, but that's the only thing I would consider."

Q3: Contextual Joy

"I knew teaching was about my love of kids. The further you move away from the classroom, the [fewer] opportunities you have to work with kids. I'm a relationship person. I love working with kids. I have the impression I'm not leaving the situation I'm in."

"I get so much satisfaction out of what happens in the classroom. The love of the [content] I'm able to share for my kids. They will use it in the future. So many kids—I feel like I've impacted life decisions made because of me and my class."

Pers<u>on</u>verance

What about you? Have you ever—even momentarily—considered moving into another role within education rather than staying as a classroom teacher? Do you know people who have? What has their experience been, and what has kept you going? For those reading who support classroom teachers and have already made this leap, what has your experience been? Are you grateful? What might have changed your decision and encouraged you to stay, if anything? With which theme does your answer most resonate—Higher Calling, Community, the Only Option, or Contextual Joy? Encouragement: Share your answer with others.

Question 4

Q4: At some point in your career, did you *actively* **consider (not a fleeting thought) switching fields or leaving teaching for another profession? If so, what kept you in the field?**

This question is all about action. The majority of veteran teachers interviewed originally said they did not actively consider leaving the field. It was clear that, even though things are challenging and there can be aspects of teaching beyond the control of the classroom teacher, most participants resolved to accept those challenges and continue persevering in a career that still suited them.

Q4: A Higher Calling

"There is so much gratification when a kid comes back and says, 'Thank you so much' or 'I hated learning math, but now I know I can do it' or 'You made me feel this way.' That's what I live for—helping kids believe in themselves or having them believe anything is possible!"

Q4: The Only Option

"I have looked into other programs, degrees, and looked at a fast-track program at [university] for nursing. Looked into that. Tried to map it out about sacrifices my family would be taking for us to be able to manage it. At the time the sacrifice ultimately came down to something I couldn't put my family through. I don't regret it."

Q4: Community

"What's kept me there is—it goes back to working with my friends. When I grew up, the mantra was, 'You will be successful, you will go to college, you will be whatever you want to be...' And when I got out into the world of education, I realized I was in the minority so relying on my friends/colleagues is what helped."

Q4: Contextual Joy

"Ultimately, I love it. The thing that has helped me stay in the profession has been me being active and moving around a little bit. I never wanted a position in education without being in the classroom, but being in a few different buildings has really helped me."

Pers<u>on</u>verance

What about you? Are you an administrator or school counselor or holding another position within education after having been a classroom teacher? What pulled you that direction? Or are you a classroom teacher who has not considered leaving the field but maybe considered another position within the field? What keeps you going as a teacher? With which theme does your answer most resonate—Higher Calling, Community, **the** Only Option, or Contextual Joy? Encouragement: Share your response with others.

Question 5

Q5: When you think about who you are as a person, tell me how you think that may relate to your longevity in the classroom?

Different from the other questions, this one asked the veteran teachers to look within themselves and call out personality traits, core values, or other aspects of their character that could have contributed to their longevity as a classroom teacher. They had the freedom to take their answers whichever way they wanted. Naturally, the four themes—Higher Calling, the Only Option, Community, and Contextual Joy—still emerged.

In general, teachers humbly describe who they are based on who they have become from their experiences as classroom teachers or who they have always been based on their family support and how they were raised. Nearly every participant gave multiple qualities that contributed to their longevity as a classroom teacher, rather than focusing on just one.

Q5: A Higher Calling

"Empathetic to my core. I feel for people a lot. I think that gets me through the day. I am much more the mom and the friend and a mentor than I am a teacher. Regardless of what happens, I can look at my kids and realize there's more to it than this. I can come back tomorrow, and it's OK—for a different reason than just teaching."

"I have faith in God; I know God has a plan in my life. He has taken care of me. I've had a lot of things happen. God put me on this planet to do something. There is someone I'm meant to influence today. That's my job."

Q5: The Only Option

"Single biggest attribute, I can genuinely say that kids bring out the best in me. Being a classroom teacher, being with high school kids day in and day out—they bring out the best in me."

Q5: Community

"I have a strong support system within my family and my work community. Those are where my friends are. That has kept me going. I'm able to roll with the punches and try not to get worked up about all the different things that come down the pike with education. It's just about the kids."

Q5: Contextual Joy

"I see myself as a lifelong learner. Being in the classroom is such a great opportunity to continue my own learning. Even though I've taught [grade and content] forever—I haven't taught it the same way every year. I am always learning new things; kids are...different. I'm always changing what I'm teaching. The state changes the curriculum, or I've changed what I'm teaching. Switching from trimesters to semesters really changed things too. That was a challenge to learn how to adapt what I taught. Having to adjust **and** adapt to going back to the nongifted learner is a challenge. I need to revise what I have to make it better suited to my students and their needs."

For this question, it is also important to highlight the top four attributes that teachers noted about themselves as they answered, across all four themes:

Q5: Optimist

"My rose-colored glasses are permanently affixed to my face. I try to be as positive as possible and stay out of the teachers' lunchroom since there's too much negative."

Q5: Compassion

"My purpose for being there is more of a passion for students, youth, and a compassion for who they are."

Q5: Perseverance

"I think I have perseverance that I'm not going to give up on a whim because I have a few tough students in a year. I want to make things better instead of quitting."

Q5: Strong Work Ethic

"I have a really strong internal work ethic, and I believe in the mission of teaching itself."

Personverance

What about you? What *internal* factors have contributed to your longevity? How do your Enneagram number, Myers-Briggs score, zodiac sign, DISC assessment score, strengths, or other traits correlate with your ability to stay in the education field, either as a classroom teacher or in another supporting role? Do you relate to any of the mentioned traits above? With which theme does your answer most resonate— Higher Calling, Community, the Only Option, or Contextual Joy? Encouragement: Share your response with others.

Question 6

Q6: When you think about the *context* **in which you have worked, are there aspects of your experience(s) that might have contributed to your longevity in the classroom?**

This question asks teachers to zoom out and look at their career on a more macro level. While Q5 focuses on *internal* factors, Q6 focuses on *external* factors. Context meant different things for different teachers like people (students and colleagues), buildings, districts, students, or community served. Naturally, this question lent itself most for veteran teachers to focus on how *context* impacted their *joy* as classroom teachers or how the people contributed to their decisions to stay.

The main comments made about context were surrounding either finding the right school or district and staying there, or knowing they were in the wrong place and working to get out of the situation rather than out of the profession entirely. The resilience shown by teachers who knew classroom teaching was still *for* them, despite their current circumstances, was most notable.

One teacher even mentioned being surprised by seeing other journeys of teachers who had been in the same place their entire careers:

"I tend to get bored, need change, diversity, variety. Need to always be learning. I am one of those people that—if I feel like I'm in a rut, I get frustrated, unhappy. I look at people who have been with this district and I wonder, 'How have you never gone anywhere else for thirty years?' Day after day, month after month, year after year, bouncing around has really been what keeps me moving. When it wasn't stimulating intellectually, I knew something would change. Often it was beyond my control, but it ended up being just what I needed."

Q6: A Higher Calling

"…That's when I learned [a family member] had cancer. Recommended to take the year off because he was going to be dead within a year. I had all the faith in the world that he would live…he didn't. I knew I was being moved [schools]. Low man on the totem pole. The teachers I worked with moved all my stuff, set up my classroom, set up two weeks of lessons. The kindness of people is so overwhelming sometimes. There is no other…kindness can change somebody's day."

Q6: The Only Option

"The atmosphere has become divided, but I know this is where I am supposed to be and what I am supposed to do."

Q6: Community

"It's very important. I don't know if I would have stayed [in teaching] if we had remained a high school of five hundred and not diverse. I have grown along with the district. The diversity—I consider that a blessing every day. I was embarrassed to come from a nondiverse community then teach in a nondiverse community. I watched the first few people of color come to [school name], and now it's a completely different place. It's like I've taught at three different schools, 26 percent nonwhite. So proud of that. I tell stories all the time about the multicultural experience here. I doubt I would have stayed if it hadn't become multicultural. Plus, all the electives. We only had a few—now there are many! We went from bare bones to this amazing university feel with dozens of electives."

Q6: Contextual Joy

"Turnover and support from administration is much different [in other schools]. There are districts I've been in that are very negative all the time. It is hard for me to be around negative people. In education, we are very type A personality people, so it doesn't take many to add others into that. In [my current district], there is a tremendous number of positive people—doesn't mean it's easy or not frustrating. I've been frustrated. The overall feeling is for the most part, you're going to see happy people that enjoy what they're doing. It's a very easy place to come to daily."

Pers__on__verance

What about you? What *external* factors have contributed to your longevity? How can you correlate your organization, community, etcetera, to the reasons you have stayed or will continue to stay? With which theme does your answer most resonate— Higher Calling, Community, the Only Option, or Contextual Joy? Encouragement: Share your response with others.

Question 7

Q7: As you reflect on your career, are there reasons you have stayed *because of* or reasons you have stayed *in spite of?*

This two-part question allowed respondents to determine whether both parts or only one was most appropriate for them to answer. The most amazing part about this question is how seven veteran teachers quickly said there was nothing they stayed in spite of, *and* every single participant had reasons they stayed because of, many of which fell into the same themes—Higher Calling, the Only Option, Community, and Contextual Joy—that had already continually emerged throughout the interview.

Q7: A Higher Calling

Because of: "I can't imagine going anywhere else. Truly. I am very comfortable in what I do and confident in what I do. I feel a part of the community—I've been there forever. Even though I don't live there, I feel a part of it. I have a history and reputation."

Q7: The Only Option

Because of: "When things get tough, I must stay for health insurance. I'm my family's health insurance, and I have a [family member] with major health concerns. That's the bottom line. I can't leave. I can't! It's not even an option."

Q7: Community

Because of: "The relationships I have here. The environment here. I feel safe, cared about. I have felt empowered being part of committees, district things. I have been given opportunities to keep my confidence. I stayed because of—I feel my administration has confidence in me, and I feel like I'm doing a good job in what I do. I feel that over the years, I've been given opportunities that demonstrate I'm doing the right thing, and I'm right where I need to be. Just one or two things that empower somebody. I normally wouldn't have been part of something, but someone brought it out of me. This is a great place to work. What's kept me is that we have a great environment here. Not a competitive environment here. I work with the best department—we share ideas, bounce off each other, always collaborating, sharing. It's hard when you're in a space where people keep things to themselves. We laugh together and can crank out some serious work together. We all *want* to work together."

In spite of: "We have had some difficult groups of kids. Not uncommon for me to be told I'm awful, expletives thrown at my face. For whatever reason, I keep telling myself it can't be like this forever."

Q7: Contextual Joy

Because of: "The love of doing it…[grade level] kids…when I first came into [this grade level], I didn't have a clue about that age, but I've grown a love for teaching them, talking to them. It's **been very enjoyable.** I'm so glad I was led to this path. No regrets!"

In spite of: "Changes in schedule, increased workload, decreased opportunities to collaborate throughout the school day. Workload."

Beyond the more common themes, one new one that emerged in the "in spite of…" portion of this question only was the idea of all the extras that teachers must endure on a daily and annual basis that few others outside of school even know about. Common teacher woes like evaluations, negative communication with the families they serve, student learning objectives, data compilation, and disciplining students with increased challenging behaviors came up often.

One teacher explained this concept succinctly: "All the extras. If you could just walk in every day and just teach—no forms, emails, professional development…that's my 'in spite of.' I wish I could just come in every day and shut my door." Nearly a dozen more participants shared similar frustrations of feeling like the demands have continued growing, while the time given to achieve them has only stayed the same or decreased.

Common barriers teachers mention they are staying *in spite of* ranged from factors not seen as much or not seen in the same way in other industries, like societal changes or perceptions of teachers and lack of support, lack of family support when working through grades or student discipline, or feeling the need to have an additional job on top of teaching to make ends meet. On the other hand, these teachers shared some factors likely found in all industries which impacted their decision-making and frustration levels, like poor experiences with leadership, bureaucracy, coworkers who are not helpful, or high turnover.

On the more positive side, teachers quickly and gladly answered all their reasons for *why* they stayed, most commonly referring to the joy they get from the classroom, their students, or their colleagues. Most did not forget to mention a practical reason too—the need to remain because of how their pay only increases as they continue throughout their careers.

Personverance

What about you? Are there reasons you have stayed *because of* or *in spite of*? List them below, and feel free to categorize them however you feel fit. See if there are patterns or if you tend to list more in one category than in the other. With which theme does your answer most resonate—Higher Calling, Community, the Only Option, or Contextual Joy? Why do you think that is? Encouragement: Share your response with others.

Now that you have had the opportunity to consider your own story and go through these questions, either alone or with a group, part 4 will look ahead to what can be done, given what we have learned and how we can all move forward with these themes in mind *and* try to make a better future for our educators, which will undoubtedly impact our students.

Part 4

Takeaways
How Do We
Help Develop
Teacherverance
and Best Support
Teachers?

Chapter 8
Implications

There is a nobility to teaching that supersedes any amount of money you make.
—**Veteran Teacher**

I think [classroom teaching] is the most important profession in the world.
—**Veteran Teacher**

The purpose of the original study was to identify common themes to see if there were any patterns in the responses of teachers who persevere and remain in the classroom. The goal was to understand the nature of teachers who persevere, finding common traits, characteristics, or circumstances that can be applied further to determine how to create conditions that will encourage teachers to stay in the field for years to come. The results of the original study suggest longevity is more likely for those who tap into a Higher Calling, have a connection to Community, feel teaching is the Only Option, or find the right Contextual Joy in which to teach.

The book you are currently reading is a way to bring these to life more than a study with some numbers and data so that it is tangible, relevant, and inspirational to any classroom teacher out there considering whether they can stay for five, ten, or twenty more years. If there is something unique about *teacherverance* in educators, the original study contributes to capturing it by identifying the common themes, patterns, and rationales for why veteran teachers report they remained in the classroom, and by documenting differences between those who have various scores on their self-perceived levels of grit test they took before the interviews. As introduced in chapter 1, the term *teacherverance*—combining *teacher* and *perseverance*—refers to the ability of a teacher to endure policy, staff, administration, societal, and cultural changes to persevere and commit to a long career serving students daily.

The four themes that emerged and became apparent in the teacher interviews were Higher Calling, Community, the Only Option, and Contextual Joy. As a result of these four consistent themes, classroom teachers and the educators and family members who support them all have a framework and language to draw upon to help continue motivation efforts. Every single teacher who participated in the original study—regardless of self-perceived level of grit—had something positive to share when asked if they could recall staying *because of* or *in spite of* various factors.

This fact alone demonstrates there are always positive aspects reflected in the responses of classroom teachers, even when it is most challenging. Conversely, teachers with higher levels of self-perceived grit had less reasons to stay *in spite of*, which is congruent with the implication of seeing fewer negatives in the first place. Additionally, it could mean they do not let these negative factors frustrate them as much as teachers with lower self-perceived levels of grit.

There may be implications in the results of this study for both teachers and administrators. For teachers, the information presented may have different implications, depending on how far along teachers are in their careers. Implications can also be for preservice teachers who may need support preparing for careers in a field marked with uncertainty, continual changes, increasing demands, and feeling underappreciated. Results of this study suggest longevity is more likely for those who tap into a Higher Calling, have a connection to Community, feel teaching is the Only Option, or find the right Contextual Joy in which to teach.

The information presented also suggests midcareer teachers may wish to do something similar. If they have considered leaving or trying something different, it might be time for them to dig deep to determine what truly is their Higher Calling. This could also be the right time to reconsider the positive or more pragmatic side of the Only Option. Midcareer teachers could determine if they have found the right Community of colleagues or how they can lean on a mentor or friend to support them. Finally, they could be reassessing their Context to determine if a change is needed. Veteran teachers, like the ones in the original study, may benefit from seeing they are not alone and being reminded of the hard times they have overcome, while recognizing the opportunity they must reach out and be mentors for the beginning and midcareer teachers.

Beyond the classroom teacher, this book and the study results have implications for school administrators as well. The words "administrator" or "administration" were mentioned *eighty-three* times in the interviews, without any specific prompting, both in a negative and a positive context. This shows the immense influence administrators can have on the experience of a classroom teacher and affirms the need to ensure their positional power is used for good.

Of course, you know best in your own heart where you are in your career, with your friends, family, and even yourself. If any of this has become emotional for you or uncovered truths about you that empower you or give you permission to leave, do so if this is what is best for you. I never have intended for this book or research to keep people in situations that are not healthy for them. If you are holding out hope and believe in the power of what you are doing—whether it is the positional power administrators might have to affect change or the power of a teacher to impact lives of their students—then keep reading for actionable steps and encouragement for how to continue in ways that serve you best.

The next section provides opportunities and ideas for teachers, administrators, or even policymakers to make the four themes—Higher Calling, Community, the Only Option, and Contextual Joy—relevant for themselves or the teachers they serve. This is in an effort to build teacher capacity to persevere through difficult challenges, societal pressures, and increasing expectations with decreasing time and resources—or *teacherverance*.

Chapter 9
Applications

What do we do with all this information? At the end of the day, teaching is *hard* no matter how connected we are to a Higher Calling, the Community, our Only Option reasoning, or what factors impact our Contextual Joy. Nobody understands this more than the classroom teachers enduring the increasing challenges and the school administrators supporting them. While I do believe there are more systemic changes that need to be made to education moving forward, these are all beyond the scope of this book.

(Some of these include discussions surrounding teacher compensation packages; respect; increased focus on standardized tests and data with decreased resources; society taking responsibility for changing family dynamics and declining mental health in students and their families; flexible and hybrid schedules for teachers, students, and school administrators to reflect the direction the rest of the world has already gone; *actual changes* to support and address school safety; increased screen time for minors and the implications it is having on an entire generation; and more expectations on teachers with seemingly fewer on students and families.)

Nevertheless, this closing section will uncover some tangible takeaways within our control, based on the four themes, in hopes of every reader connecting with at least one of them. It is not necessary to have meaningful connections with all; instead, connecting with at least one can give us newfound reasons to keep going and practice strong *teacherverance*.

Higher Calling

Classroom Teachers

While it might seem demeaning to start with platitudes regarding meditation or finding your core meaning, it is nevertheless important to consider what helps you persevere, despite the challenging circumstances you face daily. If you can tap into whatever the reason was for why you first started and revisit this reason daily, you are more likely to focus on that, while letting the frustrations come and go. There is an argument against calling teaching a Higher Calling[36] because this is how people will justify paying teachers lower or treating them poorly through systemic oversight.

However, the idea of a Higher Calling could ring true in any profession beyond this argument. For anyone who believes in a higher power or has deep connection to a particular set of beliefs or faith, it is likely they see work as something they *get* to do rather than *must* do. This important distinction is something that can keep any employee going even during frustrations, challenges, or disrespect. A Higher Calling can mean different things to different people. For some, it might be religious or spiritual; for others it might be a duty to self, students, family, or friends to create a life worth living for all. Feeling like we are *called* to be doing something completely helps shift mindsets and create a deeper sense of meaning focusing on the *internal* core of self instead of the *external* factors that are out of our control.

Administrators

If you are a school administrator reading this book, then, first of all—thank you. Thank you for being one of the good ones who cares deeply about taking care of the teachers you serve because ultimately, everything we do is for the students. But if we forget about the teachers who most directly serve the students, then we are missing a step. When we discuss a Higher Calling, it is first important to note yours. Many school administrators started in teaching and felt called to move into school leadership for a variety of reasons. You are not immune from the hard and challenging work, yet oftentimes you must set aside your own feelings, emotions, and experiences to best serve the students and staff. So don't forget about yourself and your own purpose for being in this work first.

Then, once you have identified your own Higher Calling, help teachers uncover—or be reminded of—theirs. Ask questions beyond the script of a post conference. Ask them how they are doing or feeling. Help them to remember to breathe first when teachers come to you exhausted or frustrated about something. Help remind them—and take your own advice—that we are all human trying the best we can. Provide resources—and space for teachers to use those resources—that go beyond the data, and instead discuss the depth and breadth and *heart work* we do as educators daily.

You could also start staff meetings with meaningful conversations, letting teachers know they are cared for as people and giving them time to connect on the purposeful work they are doing. If a teacher is struggling, before giving suggestions, ask questions about why they first started teaching and what is currently keeping them going. Then provide recommendations based on how they answer. Sometimes this might be a simple reminder for them about their *why*, and give them all the energy they need to persevere.

Community

Classroom Teachers

Find your community! With there being four options mentioned earlier about how to find the right fit—classroom; school; district, city, or town; or your own family or friends— there are plenty of ways to do this. It can be challenging to do this so early on in your career, since we know great teaching jobs can be hard to shop around for once you have put a lot of years in; however, notice that one of the options for community has nothing to do with where you work.

The family and friends you keep outside of school while you are a teacher have a strong correlation with your happiness and satisfaction inside of school. After all, we tell our students how important it is to find strong friends who uplift and support us; this is even more important when we are in such a demanding job, which takes so much of our energy and time. We need our family and friends to listen when helpful, encourage when we need it most, and to let us vent without question sometimes as well. We are the stories we bring home and the company we keep. If we do not surround ourselves with family and friends who help bring light and levity for us in the evenings and weekends, the days will be that much more challenging. The best part? We get to lean into these people, regardless of the school or district environment we are in.

What a gift it would be to create or settle into a community you also want to find yourself in daily. Whether it is a community you create as a teacher in the classroom with your students; the community of your department, hallway, or grade level in the school; or the larger community of the district and town in which you serve, the school community can matter and have a direct correlation on your happiness and satisfaction. The challenging part of this can be to find it early and maintain it over time.

Education is the one job in which experience can have a paralyzing effect on the growth and movement of a teacher due to pay scales making teachers too expensive to switch. Because of this, teachers either need to switch early *or* work hard to create a strong community in the environment they find themselves in long-term. This can be done through setting up staff happy hours, checking in on your colleagues, getting involved in the community outside school to meet more people serving the same area, or simply being intentional about stopping by the new colleague's room to see if they need anything.

Administrators

Create and foster a compelling community that is worth showing up for daily!

Think of creative ways you, as a leader in the building or district, can create powerful moments for your staff to engage and to feel like they are truly part of something special. If the staff feel it, the students will as well. A book many of our staff have read in my current district is *The Power of Moments*, by Chip and Dan Heath. The subtitle and message are simple: Why Certain Experiences Have Extraordinary Impact.[37] As a result, our district is intentional about creating "peak moments" that seek to *elevate*, provide deep *insight*, demonstrate *pride*, or foster *connection* among our staff and students. We discuss in meetings how to make these moments happen for our staff (and students); one example that has come out of it is something so simple as "Mug Club."

Mug Club is our catchy title for the simplest and purest of ideas: every Friday morning our entire staff is invited to start their day in the staffeteria, and the only requirement is to bring their own mugs if they want some coffee. I can take zero credit for this—it was thought of by some brilliant members of our team who saw a need for fostering a stronger community within our staff. So, the giant coffee maker was purchased and all the coffee and creamer one could want, and the rest is magic.

Every Thursday afternoon, someone from our leadership team turns the coffeepot on and sets the timer, and then by Friday morning, there is hot, freshly brewed coffee for anyone to enjoy. People come and talk about their mugs (cute and filled with stories!), their weeks, and their weekends, and simply *connect* and partake in community. There is no agenda, no attendance taken, no official start or stop time—except, of course, when the students need us in our classrooms and hallways—and it is always a full room. The only goal is to foster community, and it has accomplished that. Many of our staff stopped scheduling regular meetings on Friday due to wanting to prioritize this moment, and it has been something we all have come to plan on, look forward to, and cherish.

Another idea is something our district calls Project100. This is the goal for every student and staff member in the district (100 percent) to be connected to something inside— or outside—of the school community that brings them joy and gives them a feeling of togetherness. We are aware of the impact there is on a student's success in the classroom when they feel connected. When students participate in clubs or athletics or feel connected to something outside of school with their family, religious organization, or community group, they feel a larger sense of pride and commitment to the work they do in the classroom.

Similarly, we want to foster a school community of *staff* who equally feel connected to something, whether that is a committee, club, or sport they lead or participate in throughout the school day or something they connect with outside of school. Connected and engaged staff can also feel more success and satisfaction during school when they have other avenues to tap into their own additional passions, talents, interests, and skills beyond the content they teach. Regardless of how positive a school culture anyone has, it can never be *everything* to a staff member or student.

Ask your staff questions regarding how they feel about the community you all share. Be prepared to hear some tough answers, knowing that, hopefully, they will lead to shared engagement in creating a community you all want to serve in. Additionally, let staff come up with ideas and say *yes*—giving them the ownership and autonomy to invest in something that will provide a school community worth staying for. Again, school *can* provide a safe place for students and staff, but long-term needs to be one place they are receiving it, not the *only* place.

Contextual Joy

Classroom Teachers

It is not the role; it is where you are and what you make of it! Do not write off teaching if you have only experienced one context and are not enjoying it or not feeling truly satisfied. Say it with me again: it is not the role; it is where you are and what you make of it that truly matter. Teaching is hard everywhere. However, if we know the baseline, the common understanding is that it is hard everywhere, and if we focus on our Higher Calling, Community, Only Option reason, or *Context*, then we can better adapt to the challenges in a way that helps us persevere through it.

As someone who was in six different schools in five different school districts within the first ten years of my career, I can speak to this firsthand. I was fortunate enough to be in all high-performing schools with incredibly dedicated staff; this quickly showed me that frustrations and issues still can—and do—exist everywhere. As I navigated all the transitions early on and saw lots of ways of "doing school," I also learned there is no one right way of approaching school, students, discipline, family communication, or anything of that nature. Instead, there are lots of well-intentioned people *everywhere*, and they are all trying their best. What is most important for *you* is to find the *context*—grade level, content area, school district, community—that best serves you and your needs so that you can best serve the needs of your students, all while prioritizing yourself long-term.

As I mentioned earlier, I had a teaching job at a school I loved with people I admired. When I landed this teaching job, I felt like I had "made it" and planned on staying there forever. A series of unfortunate and unexpected events led me to experience a reduction in force and teaching—not by choice—a different subject. Again, I was in a community I loved with the most amazing staff and students. The content did not fit me or what I wanted for the rest of my life. It felt like trying to fit a square peg in a round hole.

Nobody was asking me to leave—quite the contrary. People who knew I was struggling would encourage me to stay, reminding me of how valued I was through coaching three sports, leading the pep rally events, joining district-wide committees, and running the Spirit Club with a large, diverse group of students. I *could* have stayed there forever, and I *could* still be there. Yet I knew deep down the *context* was not the right fit. In this case the *context* was the content area. Suddenly, I found myself applying to jobs outside a district I never saw myself leaving, all because I knew the importance of finding *joy* in the context.

Another spin on this Contextual Joy concept is an encouraging note for teachers who feel stuck due to not liking the context but feel like they cannot move because of how many constraints there can be around contracts and years of experience. If this is you, I encourage you to do some deeply intentional work to consider if staying is the right move (for other reasons like Higher Calling, Community, or the Only Option) and then work hard to *make* the context you are in joyful. Only pay attention to the pieces of the work that pertain to you. Surround yourself only with colleagues who bring you joy. If there are people bringing you down and you must see them daily, breathe and remember you are not going to give them any more energy than what you need to in order to be professional and do the job well.

For any teachers reading this who are blaming their issues on administration, I am sorry and even more sorry about how wronged you feel by the people who should be supporting you most. I want to encourage you and remind you that not all administrators are made the same. I would like to think we are all doing the best we can, though I know we can all let people down. It is important for you to know this: if you feel administrators are the problem, you have the wrong administrators, not necessarily the wrong career choice.

I know plenty of individual administrators and full administrative teams who would do anything for their teachers and students. They do this with genuine care and concern for others, a servant attitude, and a posture of wanting to do what is right for their entire school community. They do exist! If you need it, I am now giving you permission to find the right leaders and accept nothing less.

You can bring and receive joy in all contexts, and I hope this note gives you the encouragement and motivation you need to do so. There is nothing more sad or disappointing than new teachers who are in a tough first year or first few years, and they leave rather than trying out teaching in another school, grade level, or content area. This is because they are giving up on the profession because of one context when we know it is not the role; it is where you are and what you make of it that truly matter.

Administrators

While I hope *you* are also able to find the right context that brings you the most joy, it is similarly important to help create a context that sparks joy in the staff and students who join you daily. If teachers are not thriving—and therefore not serving the students well—partner with them to provide the resources or time they need to be better prepared, or ask them if they are in the right context. It is not always easy, though sometimes it truly can be as simple as switching teacher content areas or grade levels, if that is something you can do within the schedule.

After focusing on helping teachers find the right context for themselves, work on creating a context full of *joy* for all of you. Think through peak moments you and your team can create—working within your budget and time constraints, of course—that can help bring joy for everyone. Let the staff dress casually if that is what they want. Say "yes" to the simple requests when you are able. Have open-door opportunities to truly listen to what your staff's needs and wants are. Then make changes to demonstrate that you are action oriented, and it is not a show.

One year the principal I worked with invited all staff to meet with him for a one-on-one meeting and asked the same questions of each staff member who took him up on this offer: What is something you are proud of? What is one quick switch that would make your day better? While some teachers enjoyed the free liberties of the latter question and had fun with their answers (margarita machine, anyone?), one intervention teacher quickly shared their frustration with having an advisory student group, while many other teachers in a similar position did not, due to their need to meet with students and strategize with teachers to plan across content areas and grade levels during that time. This was an oversight on the administrative team, where they truly had just not thought through this level of detail. Therefore, the principal heard the concern and quickly problem-solved so the teacher would no longer have an advisory group the rest of the year, effective within a week of that meeting.

This was an administrator who cared about the context for their teachers and was willing to work swiftly and eagerly to help care for them and remove any barriers keeping them from accessing the joy of the job. Even better, the teacher who took over her advisory did so by choice and with excitement, when asked, because she saw it as a unique way to connect with students she typically would not have otherwise seen throughout the day. A win-win situation!

As the school administrator, you have the power to create the type of environment students and staff *want* to come to every day. Haim G. Ginott was a schoolteacher, child psychologist, and psychotherapist as well as a parent educator. One of his most famous quotes for teachers was all about the impact they have on the classroom:

> *"I've come to a frightening conclusion that I am the decisive element in the classroom. It's my personal approach that creates the climate. It's my daily mood that makes the weather. As a teacher, I possess a tremendous power to make a child's life miserable or joyous. I can be a tool of torture or an*

instrument of inspiration. I can humiliate or heal. In all situations, it is my response that decides whether a crisis will be escalated or de-escalated and a child humanized or dehumanized."

If teachers are the decisive element in the classroom, I would like to extend Ginott's thinking here to the influence school administrators can have on entire schools or districts. I have given myself the liberty to rewrite this. If you are a school administrator, feel free to take a picture of this as a reminder or to print it out for your desk or laptop:

I've come to a frightening conclusion that I am the decisive element in the [school or district]. It's my personal approach that creates the climate. It's my daily mood that makes the weather. As a school administrator, I possess a tremendous power to make a [teacher's or child's or guardian's] life miserable or joyous. I can be a tool of torture or an instrument of inspiration. I can humiliate or heal. In all situations, it is my response that decides whether a crisis will be escalated or de-escalated and a [child, their parent, or a teacher] humanized or dehumanized.

Joy in school is still possible, despite the added challenges and increased behaviors we see. Hire mentally strong, resilient teachers who are excited to be there and add value to the work you are doing. Take care of them, and help them to find joy in the context you all share.

The Only Option

Classroom Teachers

Remember there are two sides here. One side is the positive or inspirational. The other side is more pragmatic with a hint of desperation. First, identify which camp you fall into. Be honest! While you do not need to tell anyone out loud, it is at least helpful to be honest with yourself on where you fall.

Have you always wanted to be a teacher and could not imagine yourself doing anything else? Is teaching the Only Option because you feel a sense of obligation, duty, and satisfaction in the work you are doing? There is a connection with Higher Calling here too. Maybe you are someone who feels compelled to teach because you know you are shaping another generation, and you feel affirmed of being in the business of growing people. Even though the days have ups and downs, you feel a steadiness of knowing you are on the right path for you, and no other career could help fulfill it.

If this is the case for you, rest assured you are doing meaningful work—and keep it up! Consider being a mentor for early-career teachers and helping lead the work in your building so other teachers still trying to find their ways have someone like you to learn from and aspire to be. It is not that you are perfect; it is simply that there is a level of assuredness that you are doing exactly what you were made to do. An incredible feeling. Relish in it, keep doing it, and help others come alongside you to create a community of people doing what they were all created for!

If this is not the case for you, are you able to be honest with yourself enough to recognize you fall more in the Only Option on the more pragmatic and desperate side? I know this can be difficult to acknowledge, but we know acknowledging is the first step to improving or finding a better situation. Lean into the support you have, and if you do not have any support in the school, work to find it outside of school. Receive love from friends and family, and look for ways to tap into a Higher Calling or stronger purpose for your *why*, beyond merely feeling stuck. You could also engage in your Community or change Contexts to reveal more Joy.

Regardless of which type of Only Option speaks to you, it is important to know which side you are on and how it impacts your perspective of your school day and your interactions with colleagues, students, and their families. Teachers who see teaching as the Only Option in a positive or inspirational way are the ones you want to have on your team and in your corner. If that is you, please let your light shine. Conversely, teachers who see teaching as the Only Option in a pragmatic or desperate way are not to be written off. If that is you, please know I believe you still have a lot to offer, and I hope you can find the support to bring out the best in yourself while you are continuing to serve as a teacher daily.

Administrators

Considering the duality of the Only Option would be imperative to help provide support for varied teacher needs. Take care of *both* types of teachers; do not overlook either group. The ones staying for inspirational and positive reasons need to feel uplifted, supported, and valued. They often want to know they are doing a good job, even though they will keep doing a good job regardless. The most common misconception surrounds assuming they are always okay. Just because you have teachers who are consistent, strong, thorough, and who will do anything you ask them to simply because they *want* to be there, this does not mean they are immune to hard days that leave them also questioning their career decisions.

The ones staying for reasons out of desperation need to feel valued, supported, and cared for because doing so helps the entire school community—the teachers themselves as well as the students and families they serve. Very rarely do burned-out or jaded teachers start in the profession feeling this way. Therefore, ask them questions about why they started; lean into tough—yet helpful—conversations about *how* their perceptions and energy toward the profession have changed.

If teachers have been around for at least five or ten years, it is a completely different profession than when they first signed up. Imagine veteran teachers with even more experience. Value their experience, and engage them in ways they can find other means of *teacherverance* by helping them uncover their own Higher Calling, getting them more involved in the Community, or helping them find the right Context. They sometimes have "seen it all," and the historical context they can provide can be invaluable in the organization of a school. Leverage it, and help them feel like their voices matter just as much as you are helping the students feel like theirs do too.

Chapter 10
Conclusion

We first examined the historical data to support the need for this information on teacher perseverance to be more widespread because we can all agree we are at an inflection point in public education—from teachers of all experience levels looking to leave (or actually leaving), to significantly fewer teachers entering the profession in the first place with undergraduate education programs reporting continually decreasing numbers.[38]

Then, we looked at the four major themes emerging from the original study three years ago with over forty veteran teacher participants:

- **Higher Calling:** Feeling a sense of awe, spiritual awakening, faith, or otherness as a classroom teacher remains in the field for reasons beyond the classroom, the students, or the school.

- **Community:** Four pathways of how veteran teachers experienced community:

  o With their students

  o With their colleagues

  o With the overall community of the district, town or city

  o With friends or mentors outside of school

- **The Only Option:** This includes a duality of two sides of responses:

  o *Positive/Inspiration:* Enthusiasm exudes a sense of calm, duty, and purpose as teachers know they cannot imagine doing any other role, despite its challenges.

  o *Pragmatic/Desperation:* Focusing on the necessity of teaching due to the consistent and predictable pay raises, job security, and strong insurance and benefits for their families. This side is where teachers admit the necessary role this job plays and their inability to feel comfortable taking a risk to find something else at the time of frustration.

- **Contextual Joy:** Finding joy in what they do as classroom teachers based on the appropriate contextual factor at the appropriate time in the right environment—school building, the right leadership team, or enjoyment of the town or city or students they have taught.

This was all in a way to capture the *teacherverance* these veteran teachers have demonstrated throughout their careers to uncover tips for teachers and school administrators. *Teacherverance* is defined as the ability of a teacher to endure policy, staff, administration, and societal and cultural changes to persevere and commit to a long career serving students daily.

Next, we looked at the various questions used to get to these four themes so that you, as the reader, could also have time to reflect on each theme and question. You could even take the Grit Scale Survey from Dr. Duckworth's research by going to her website.*This section helped personalize the experience by having readers answer questions in the appropriate Pers<u>on</u>verance sections so you could think critically about what the other veteran teachers experienced compared to your own experiences, while reading some of my own too. These sections highlighted how a person can show perseverance through sharing their own personal story.

Finally, there were specific applications and implications shared based on these four themes. Separate for school administrators and teachers, they were shared to give tangible action steps for any reader in these roles, regardless of how many years of experience they have. The goal here is that after reading this book, you will feel equipped to support yourself as the classroom teacher, or the classroom teachers as an administrator. We can talk all we want about the teacher shortage, but focusing on the ones who stay is where the real magic comes in. The ones who stay are the ones who impact the lives and legacies of students, families, and entire communities. The ones who stay are the ones who focus on their own Higher Callings, sense of Community, Only Option, or Contextual Joy, which help them to have the highest levels of *teacherverance*.

---

* https://angeladuckworth.com/grit-scale/

Bonus Chapter!

Teaching is hard, *and* teaching is joyful, fulfilling, and necessary for an active, informed, educated, and ever-changing society. How do we reconcile these two feelings? And what about the veteran teachers who participated in the original study? It's been three years; what are they up to now? All educators can agree that the fall of 2020 (when the original study occurred) looked very different from the fall of 2023 (when this book was written), so now it is time to finally return to updates on many of the teachers who are quoted in the previous chapters. I reached out to all forty-four participants, and while I did not hear from everyone, I did learn that 77 percent of the ones who did respond are still classroom teachers. While I am happy to report such a high retention number, this still means we lost nearly a quarter of the veteran teachers who responded in a short three years.

Since this story is so connected to my own educational journey, I also reached out to most of my own teachers—grades kindergarten through senior year of high school—whom I could track down. Even though I graduated nearly twenty years ago and, naturally, did not get to everyone, I was nevertheless encouraged to learn that a staggering 85 percent of my own teachers are still classroom teachers. This bonus chapter will examine the responses of these original participants and my own teachers after this check-in happened while writing this book and will connect their responses with the four themes we have discussed. Additionally, we will revisit Zach's story from the introduction of the book to learn what he is up to now, and we will finish with the urgency of the larger need we have as a society to embrace classroom teachers and support them at any cost.

An Update from the Original Participants of the Study: Three Years Later

I shared with the participants the results of the study and the four themes emerging, thanks to their honest feedback and input. I then asked them to comment on Higher Calling, Community, the Only Option, and Contextual Joy from their perspectives now. More than half connected their current experiences to Higher Calling and Community.

For Higher Calling, one teacher shared, "I have always felt that I was meant to be a teacher. I remember the teachers who I thought just showed up for a paycheck, and I wanted to 'save' kids from teachers like that. I also genuinely like my students! I can find several traits about each student that I like or admire." This spoke to their focus on other pieces of the work rather than the frustrating changes that have occurred over time.

Another teacher who shared about how specific roles help them stay through finding a Higher Calling by supporting and onboarding new teachers. They said, "Teaching was my love, my passion. Forty-two years was enough time in the classroom. My additional tasks in the district were fostering participation in mentoring and onboarding all new teachers, preparing them to receive their licenses. Three of us did this for several years, and it was a deeply rewarding project."

Additionally, some other teachers focused on the long-term heart of teaching. One said, "I teach to impact kids in the hopes that they build their self-belief. This is not always seen in the year I have them in class, but nothing is more valuable than when a former student shares their journey of success and happiness." Another shared a similar sentiment with, "I enjoy working with young adults as they get ready for the next chapter in their life and feel a sense of purpose, which is very gratifying personally and professionally." This helps to keep everything in perspective and not let the daily minutiae get in the way of the overall purpose. One teacher put it simply: "I love being in my classroom with my students. All the outside things we must focus on now take some of the joy away, but when I come in and teach, I love my job."

For Community—the other high percentage reporting— veteran teachers shared specifically about the importance of Community they feel with their students and their colleagues. One of the teachers who mentioned the connection with their students helped strengthen their own sense of Community shared, "I feel like I connect with my students. I believe that I have a role to play in their lives; not just as their teacher, but also as someone who can be a model, someone who listens, someone who cares."

For Community with colleagues, staff members noted the depth and longevity of relationships making all the difference. One teacher noted:

"I enjoy the community or 'family' I have with many teachers I teach alongside. Many teachers in my building opened this building [twenty years ago]. We have watched pregnancies and births, our children grow up, go off to college, get married, have kids of their own! It is such a wonderful feeling to love the people I work with as a family."

This teacher went on to acknowledge this familial sense was what kept them going on the hardest of days or season.

Another teacher was proud to share: "Our community of educators are amazing, and there is a feeling of 'being in it together' with both staff and administration." They admitted it "wasn't always the case but has been for many years now," which speaks to the strength in staying, flexing the resilience muscle, and seeing challenging seasons through. Finally, one veteran teacher shared simply: "Relationships continue to be what keeps me positive and afloat, especially when surrounded by negativity [in education]."

The next connected themes by the veteran teachers who had originally participated in the study were equally the Only Option—Positive/Inspiration side—and Contextual Joy as just under half of them reported connections to these. For Contextual Joy, one teacher shared that since our initial interviews three years ago, they are still teaching but not in the same content, which also tapped into their Higher Calling:

"I found that my calling was still in teaching but not as a classroom teacher. There was a bit of desperation in realizing that I couldn't possibly teach for a thirty-fifth year in the classroom. Luckily, I was able to find a position as an ESL teacher (having earned my TESOL [Teaching English to Speakers of Other Languages] endorsement a few years prior). I felt called to do this to support the ELL [English Language Learners] students in my classroom year after year. It has been a joy to work with [these students], their families, and their classroom teachers for these past couple of years. I have been fortunate to stay in education in a position that still has its frustrations but brings me such joy and pride in what I do for a living."

Talk about a teacher who has been able to find the right *context* to bring them more *joy*!

Another veteran teacher shared this sentiment by revealing: "Changing buildings/districts can make a big difference. Although we are ultimately in this profession to make a positive impact on kids, we can do this more successfully when we are working in a positive environment in terms of colleague positivity, administration support, and discipline consistency." One more teacher who connected their feelings to Higher Calling, Contextual Joy, *and* the Only Option in a Positive way said:

"I'm in my thirtieth year of teaching, so by definition I'm able to retire but…I still enjoy teaching and the connections that I make with a new cohort of students each fall. I concur, it is a demanding job, and the demands placed on teachers have increased exponentially since I began my career. Lastly, I admit I have been lucky throughout my career, having gotten hired in progressively 'better' working environments."

Again, if you have not found these factors yet for what "better" means to you, I encourage you to remember: it is not the role; it is where you are and what you make of it that truly matter.

An Update from My Own K–12 Teachers: Twenty to Thirty Years Later

I loved hearing from my own teachers who shaped me along the way. Born into a family0 0of educators, I was one of those who always knew I wanted to be a teacher. These amazing professionals never once had me questioning my decision. I heard from many incredible teachers, including the ones who met me early on—my first, second, and third grade teachers—to the ones who helped me through recommendation letters and college applications—my high school teachers—to everything in between. I am fortunate to be standing on the shoulders of talented, committed, and gifted educators, many of whom are still contributing to the field twenty to thirty years after I met them.

Contextual Joy was referenced as these teachers shared the importance of staying where they did over their career and how it helped set them up for success even after retiring from long, fruitful careers. One declared not only the importance of Context but also Community and how focusing on a Higher Calling can also help promote a perspective focused on what matters most:

"Building community with students, staff, and all those who work in schools is a vital part of the successes of a school district and school. Also, making sure that one doesn't take anything personally helps tremendously. I have recommended and bought the book *The Four Agreements* to help give perspective to teachers and students about their role and responsibilities to all people in schools or even in our life's journey. I worked in [a previous district] for fifteen wonderful years, and I learned a lot about myself and teaching students at risk and those who are ready to learn."

This same teacher became an administrator only a few years after I had her, and she shared, "There were a few years that I was asked to apply for the administrative position. I wanted to stay with my students because I enjoyed it so much." I am eternally grateful for her staying true to her "why" while I was there since I got to benefit from having her as a teacher for three separate classes over two different school years and from a lifetime of keeping in touch with her as a mentor.

One of my elementary teachers retired and continued as an educational consultant for neighboring schools in her retirement. She talks about the transcendence of the work and how it is a Higher Calling by saying that now, "I have the opportunity to learn and grow as an educator and strive to help teachers solve the complex problems they face. I truly feel that I am serving and giving back to the profession that has been my life's work." How grateful I am to have had someone like her building into me as a third-grade student!

Another nod to Higher Calling came from my second-grade teacher, who is still in education, though not as a classroom teacher. She is now a media center specialist serving an entire school in the same district I attended. We both always wanted to be teachers, and she went one step further to say:

"It seemed like more of a vocation than a job. I had an inner drive that motivated me to be creative, kind, and motivating to every child that was placed in my classroom. It was never about the paycheck. It was always about the smiles, hugs, and growth that I witnessed in students. When the obstacles came, they were usually in the form of discouraging words from those *outside* of the profession...they just did not understand the joy that came from making a difference."

Again, I recognize how fortunate I was to be built into by these incredibly dedicated and passionate teachers who are still serving the profession.

Suggestions, Reality Checks, and Recommendations

While most veteran teachers from the original study and my own K–12 teachers had positive memories, ideas, and shared experiences, there were still some who were honest in suggesting changes they see need to be made. The Only Option in a pragmatic/desperate way was shared by one of my former teachers when she admitted the following:

"This is my twenty-eighth year of teaching. I am at the point that I feel like even though I have always wanted to be a teacher and have enjoyed my career, I could see myself exploring other related career options. A change seems like it could be good. Unfortunately, at this point, I am in a position that I will need to finish my career in education because I am too vested in the retirement system. I want to be clear— teaching has always been my passion. Even after having completed a master's degree in administration, I have always chosen to teach. I do feel like my calling is to have an impact on the lives of my students. I just wish that in today's world, teachers were more valued and that we could have greater autonomy. These changes over the course of my career have taken some of the joy out of an otherwise rewarding career."

Knowing her, this makes me particularly sad because I know how much she has poured into her craft. She takes her job seriously, loves her students well, and should not be ending her career feeling this way. We can do better as a society to help our teachers feel valued, even up until retirement, grateful for the time they have put into helping hundreds or even thousands of students throughout their career.

On the other hand, I was excited to see one of my incredible elementary teachers, who is now retired, offer support to the system: "When I hear of so many new teachers leaving the teaching industry, I worry not enough is being done to support the emotional needs of this next generation of educators. Maybe an additional resource of positive former/retired educators could offer that hand up so sorely needed." This brings us back to the purpose of the original study.

Why are we spending all our time focusing on the teacher shortage and the teachers who are leaving? Why are we not, instead, giving a voice to the veteran teachers who are persevering or retiring after their full years of service to see how they can help contribute to the narrative that it is possible—and worth it—to stay? Remember the teacher from the original study in the previous section who shared how rewarding it was to help new teachers receive their licenses? This teacher is now retired and could still be helping if districts see the value in continuing relationships with veteran teachers beyond their retirement.

Speaking of the original study participants, there were a few who admitted to feeling stuck after three more years of teaching since I had interviewed them. They commiserate on feeling like now teaching is the Only Option in a pragmatic/desperate way. One spoke to the reality they are faced with:

"There does come a point where, even if you wanted to change districts, you can't. All schools are becoming broke, and no one is looking for an expensive teacher option. And yes, when you've invested over twenty years into a retirement system, it seems crazy to just throw that away.

Other options than teaching are extremely rare and almost never financially sensible."

Is this really the best we can do for our teachers who build into *every other* profession?

The most veteran teacher I interviewed is sixty-three years old and disclosed he passed up his district's retirement incentive eleven years ago: "I would probably retire if I had some money in the bank or if healthcare were affordable, but since neither are true, I have stuck with teaching." Additionally, he went on to say it has generally been an "easy decision since I enjoy most workdays, and my students are respectful and nice." However, he now is feeling increasingly more out of touch with students annually due to the "students' increased love of cell phone games and social media and their lack of interest in interacting with me or each other."

That final sentiment is shared by educators everywhere. The world outside of schools cannot fully comprehend what educators see daily—the addictive behaviors of students raised on screens. This addiction makes it nearly impossible for teachers of every generation to connect, manage behaviors, or make learning remotely relevant for students with access to every ounce of information they would ever want to or need to know.

The other side of feeling stuck can simply be out of lack of opportunity. One teacher was honest enough to admit, "I have attempted to move into a leadership role for several years but feel stonewalled by the district. I can't take a pay cut so teaching in a different district at this point is not possible. I am willing to change districts if it means assuming a leadership role, so I continue to actively seek out opportunities on nearly a daily basis." This is where a strong school administrator should come in, meet with the teacher, and talk about at least one of the following items:

1) Why is this teacher not getting hired in a new role in the same district? Honesty is key here, for everyone's sake.

2) What can the school administrator do to help create a better context for this teacher if it is true they will not be considered for the new role? Could that teacher be more satisfied in a different grade level or content area, or take on additional leadership roles through a supplemental rather than an actual title change?

A disgruntled teacher who feels stuck is not helpful to any school community and can—and should—still be supported.

One of the veteran teachers from the original study had since retired after a legendary career of thirty-six years serving students as a classroom teacher. He shared how all themes apply to him, for better or for worse. He knew that students noticed he talked with and cared for *everyone*. Imagine a teacher like him, who started college learning what a computer was and retiring in the past three years.

Like anyone in any profession for so long, the profession he entered after college is *completely different* than what it was when he retired. *Everything* has changed. What did not change, this teacher shared, was the "cycle we are in through education where it kept coming back around. All the same." As a result, he became frustrated by the bureaucracy;

also, he was "finished with teaching parents how to parent, which is what it became"—another reality those outside of education cannot necessarily relate to.

This veteran teacher now serves students as a paraprofessional—or teacher's aide—in his retirement and loves "not being so in charge of everything." He connects to all four themes the study uncovered, thanks to people like him who contributed their experience. See below for some of his thoughts on each theme:

- **Higher Calling.** "I always knew there was more to life than teaching, so I never let the frustrating parts that got to everyone else get to me."

- **Community.** "The community of my colleagues are what got me through everything. They lifted me up when I was down and helped me in some of the toughest moments for me and my family, especially when I was out [of the classroom, home taking care of them]."

- **The Only Option (Positive and Inspirational).** "Nothing else I would have ever wanted to do! Being called 'coach' or 'teacher' and literally changing the trajectory of people's lives is profound."

- **Contextual Joy.** "Loved doing [grade level and content] and nothing else. I was not meant to be an Advanced Placement teacher, so the context was right for me."

This is the kind of teacher we need to keep around, to build into, to listen to, and to help shape a future generation of teachers, who will then help shape a future generation of students.

Zach's Update

Remember Zach from the beginning of the book? We first were introduced to him as a teacher up until 2019. Now, four years later, he is no longer teaching and instead works in marketing and leads a group—or a movement, rather—of teachers who are *actively* seeking to leave the profession. He and his wife started the group in 2019 because, as former teachers, they wanted to create a community of people who were trying to find their way after leaving what had become their identity for so long. Their *Life After Teaching* community is now a Facebook group of over one hundred thousand members. There are roughly three million teachers in the United States. Their website and group are built to connect like-minded teachers who are seeking options outside of the traditional classroom to leverage their skills and find jobs in the marketplace or run their own businesses.

When I asked Zach about the heart behind their work, he shared they ultimately want to *not* have to exist. He and his wife dream of a world where educators are valued for their expertise and contributions to society. So they will strengthen their efforts by eventually equipping school administrators and policymakers with tools needed to help make this dream a reality. For now, however, they have found surprising growth in the four short years since they started—exacerbated by a global pandemic nobody saw coming when they began in 2019—and created a community of people encouraging one another in the endless opportunities that exist with their already-strong skill set of teaching and becoming content experts.

One of the resources Zach and his team provide to the entire community is what they call the "Ultimate Life After Teaching Job Title List." This is a sixty-six-page document averaging four to five new careers per page that actual teachers they know from the community have transitioned to as they left the industry. In it, they outline the job title, description, average salary range, and skills that are useful in each field. I cannot help but wonder how many other professions have similar resources, equipping people with tools for when they are ready to leave as a way of assuming there will come a time you will have had enough.

The salary portion is specific to one of the reasons Zach left originally. Besides going through a health scare with his wife and a real safety threat with his students, he also learned that as a newer teacher in his district, he was only making about $8,000 less than a veteran teacher in his district who was a year away from retiring. All three of these reasons were progressive wake-up calls for him that something had to change.

When I connected with Zach about his experiences and shared with him the takeaways of this book, he immediately connected with all four themes. Particularly, he noted that in such a large Facebook community of teachers who are actively considering leaving the *Community* of the school—whether the community consists of colleagues or administrators or surrounding districts or towns—really does matter. Therefore, it is paramount to provide new teachers with adequate support so they feel surrounded by the necessary community to support them.

Zach also mentioned seeing the Higher Calling connection in the Facebook group often. He agreed there is a paradox here. Following a Higher Calling in any job should never mean you are burned out and taken advantage of. It should ultimately mean it is providing you such fulfillment and purpose that you want to *keep* doing it. Zach mentioned he thinks sometimes teachers put up with a lot due to the Higher Calling concept, which is not always healthy.

Finally, Zach connected with the Contextual Joy theme, both personally and after seeing the tens of thousands of teachers trying to find better situations in different contexts. For him, he stayed in the same city in his seven years of teaching but switched between public, charter, and private, as well as content areas between grades six through eight. This way, he knew he had given every possible context a try to know that teaching was not going to be the job that sustained him throughout the rest of his career. He has also watched plenty of other teachers try switching contexts to find the right one before they consider what they really should do long-term. I wonder what teachers like Zach would have done with such a framework to make these decisions more clearly before deciding to leave.

Closing

One might say Zach, his wife, and I are on the same mission, coming from different angles. While they are trying to support the ones who are leaving and the system, I have written this book as a way to equip and encourage the ones who are staying. Like Zach, I hope teaching changes so much over the years that the concepts driving the need for this book are eventually irrelevant. That one day a child might see it and ask their guardian about a book on teacher perseverance with complete confusion while the guardian explains a time when teachers were undervalued and overworked and were afterthoughts of society. That when the guardian speaks of this time that no longer exists, the child is grateful things have changed since they know the value of the teachers in their life.

Part 1 of this book explored the background of how educators even got to the place they are in now and what has been done in the past to try and help fix it. Part 2 then shared the results of the study this work is based on and defined the themes found—Higher Calling, Community, the Only Option, and Contextual Joy. Then, readers had the opportunity in part 3 to consider their own stories and go through questions asking them to think more deeply about their own experiences around education. As we close in part 4, we have looked ahead to what can be done, given what we have learned, and how we can all move forward with these themes in mind *and* try to make a better future for our educators, which will undoubtedly impact our students.

My hope for those of you who made it this far into the bonus chapter feel like you have left with a stronger sense of your own "why" for staying in education or ways to help support those in your life who are still teaching. By uncovering our Higher Calling, leaning into our Community, staying true to our Only Option, and working to find Contextual Joy, teachers everywhere can feel empowered and motivated to stay, rather than stuck or seeking other options.

The urgency is there. The unfortunate reality of how many talented teachers are feeling was shared best by a veteran teacher from the original study who is now no longer teaching. She is consulting and serving local school districts as a coach. While it is still valuable work, we cannot afford to ignore or dismiss the feelings she—and so many others— have that lead them to leave classroom teaching. If we do not, I fear this downward spiral will only exponentially grow and leave our school systems empty of teachers who *choose* to be there. She was a veteran teacher who was incredibly talented, committed, and even a department leader at one point. Here are her reflective and honest thoughts, when asked about her three-year update:

> *There were many factors that influenced my decision to leave the classroom. I reached a point where my passion and creativity were stifled by the demands of standardized tests. I felt like my district was moving toward cookie-cutter teachers who all did the same thing at the same time. I could no longer teach the way I wanted to teach because I was the minority in a department that wanted to teach from a box curriculum.*

I used to love to incorporate creativity, project based, and hands-on learning in my room. I used to love sharing books with kids and inspiring the love of reading for enjoyment and pleasure. We just didn't do that anymore. The district was more concerned with getting 90 percent passage on the state test than they were with producing lifelong learners who love to read. I tried to apply for different jobs within the district, but I never got any of those positions. I didn't have the opportunity to grow my skills in a different capacity. I was trapped.

I had seventeen years of teaching and a master's, plus forty-five additional credit hours. The only way for me to leave to go to another district at an educator-level role was to take a massive pay cut. That's even if a district was willing to interview me with so much experience, which they weren't.

Adding to all of that were the factors of trying to navigate being in a classroom in a post-pandemic world. We had spent at least two years preaching the need for self-care and balance. The minute the pandemic was behind us, all of those beliefs went out the window. Again, teachers were asked to do more and more and more with less and less and less. Behavior occurrences with students were more frequent and more severe. Parental opposition was more vocal. And overall work ethic from students was plummeting. The apathy, entitlement, and disrespect were too much for me to handle in addition to my already desperately deflated emotional state.

Now that I'm out of the classroom, I look back, and I can't believe I lived that way for so long. Without a doubt, teachers have the most demanding jobs in the world. They are asked to do way more than is humanly possible. I say this somewhat in jest, but I feel like I'm free. I feel like I can have a life. I don't have to choose between being good at my job and being a present and active mother. Now, I can grow professionally, feel like a decent mother, and be a good friend. Since I've left the classroom, I've been given back a life.

Why and how have we become a society content with teachers feeling this way? Adding to their plates instead of taking off them. Telling them what to do instead of listening to what needs to be done. It is also easy to dismiss certain feelings when you do not know the teachers, but if you knew this teacher above, you would *want* your child in her class. You would do everything to keep her as a classroom teacher if you were the school administrator supporting her. Being in her classroom was pure magic. I am at least glad the industry did not lose her, and she found a new job consulting and coaching teachers who are still in the thick of it.

Beyond Zach and his wife's work, there are dozens of other groups with the same intent. One is specific to the United Kingdom, called *Life After Teaching: Exit the Classroom and Thrive*, which has over 150,000 members and points out this is not a uniquely American problem. Even the title suggests teachers are *not* thriving *until* they leave the classroom. Again, I ask, why are we content with this? How can we make strategic shifts to help change the narrative teachers are currently faced with?

The answer is not: "You, teachers, need to love kids more and build relationships." This minimizes and dismisses the actual issues at hand. The answer is not: "You, teachers, need to be grateful for what you have and keep in mind all workplaces have their frustrations." While every workplace does have its frustrations, this equates what teachers experience with what everyone else experiences, and it is simply not true or equitable. There is no other workplace that takes care of everyone else's children while also counseling them, parenting them, disciplining them, cheering for them, guiding them, coaching them, and listening to them, and one more thing—teaching them oftentimes based on weighty, convoluted, and ever-changing standards and expectations.

The answer is building more supportive systems and thinking more intentionally about how we view education as an entity in our society. The answer is passing laws, providing funds, and equipping teachers with the same support they equip our students with daily—time, money, and respect. Until these answers are provided, I hope this book has offered anyone reading with the strength to keep going, knowing that you are not alone and the work you do matters, makes a difference, and is *necessary* due to the impact you have on entire generations and communities.

Teachers: I hope you find your Higher Calling. I hope you feel connected to a Community that lifts you up, celebrates you, and believes in you. I hope you stay true to the Only Option concept with conviction and motivation. I hope you find the right Context that brings you Joy *or* that you can find ways to make Joy happen, wherever you already find yourself.

School administrators: I hope you can help support teachers better by at least connecting with one of these themes for them and maybe you, as well. I hope if you have influence over policy changes, you are able to make the connections with people from your own district to local universities at the state or even federal levels, to help sound the alarm in appropriate ways about what you are seeing, hearing, and feeling and how workplace conditions can improve for the teachers you serve.

The following are quotes from teachers who participated in the original study, some of which you have already seen in this book. I hope their words inspire you as they did me when I was first interviewing them.

"I genuinely love what I do. I love seeing the kids do well, what happens after they leave and come back. I've had kids invite me to their weddings, thank me for what I did. We are tasked with doing something that is more important than ever. Kids need good teachers more than they ever needed them. They need human interaction more than ever because they are getting less of it. The phones, technology, etcetera. There is going to come a moment—people are going to realize what has happened—human interaction matters most. I do what I do because I love the feeling of helping them, the feeling of 'Thank you, you helped me find (or not find) a passion.'"

"We all have those moments—those aha moments when you get the opportunity to share that joy of recognition. The 'I know this!' face is a magical experience. It keeps you going! I have more fun now than I did thirty years ago! I might be the most veteran person in the building. I have had the opportunity to be led by former students. I get to see people [as adults] every day that I knew when they were younger [as students]. If you're enthusiastic, teaching helps keep you young. I am the youngest person in the room, at least in my heart. Those of us who choose to stay—that's the reason why. There is this horrible cliche—'Those who can, do. Those who can't, teach.' There have always been so many intelligent, caring, skilled people who *choose* to teach. Not because they *can't* but because they *wanted to.*"

Finally, some teachers put it simply:

"There is a *nobility* to teaching that supersedes any amount of money you make."

"I don't think there's a more important profession on the planet. Not everybody can have an education. I love teaching. I think it's the most important profession in the world."

Just when you might think we can only get the encouragement we need from teachers, allow me to end with an article from a high school student for her school newspaper. After all, the students are a driving motivation for us in our careers![39]

"I am so stressed out."

Walking the halls of [my school], it is almost im-possible not to hear this phrase. I have used it a fair number of times in just the last week. On top of regular activities, there is no doubt that finals, end-of-course (EOC) exams, and Advanced Placement

(AP) exams induce quite a bit of stress for students. It is the end of the year, and after almost **10** *months of academics, extracurriculars, time management struggles, and sleep deprivation, we are all looking forward to a break. Senioritis has officially hit for the graduating class, and summer cannot come sooner.*

However, often forgotten, especially this time of year, are teachers. Behind every assignment we turn in is a teacher who has to grade our work. Behind every complaint about how much work we have is a teacher who has to decide how to finish teaching all of the content before the end of the school year. Behind every class activity we do is a teacher who brainstormed the most effective way to engage their students. Sure, our end of year tests are stressful, but are they not for our teachers as well? They not only have to prepare students for these tests, but also manage students' and parents' complaints, schedule changes, grading, standards from administration and their own lives, which may include a plethora of other factors. It is so easy to antagonize our teachers, but should we really be blaming them?

Teachers carefully plan their course content to fit across the school year. They have less than **180** *days to get all of the information to students before the AP test or final exam. However, with snow days, absences, and other issues that may get in the way of a lesson plan, following a previously planned agenda is not always possible.*

*In addition, teachers also have to manage behavior in their classroom, and anyone who has met high schoolers would know that getting a rowdy group of **30** teenagers to calm down and focus on something is no simple feat. Individual students' needs may require teachers to implement additional intervention. Teachers are expected to identify and assist students who may need more help, whether academic, personal, or otherwise. Many students rely on their teachers to be mentors, role models, and listening ears. Whether we see it or not, teachers play a wide range of roles in the school, and it is hard to deny the amount of effort they put into simply making sure all their students are okay.*

Grading is another element of teaching we may not always acknowledge: for every one essay we write, our teachers likely have hundreds more to grade. Getting these grades back to students, providing quality feedback, and doing so in a timely and efficient manner, is not always easy. On top of this, I cannot imagine what it must be like for teachers to constantly hear students nag about their grades when I, as a student myself, already get fed up with the never-ending academic comparison.

Teachers are also expected to write letters of recommendation for their students, an additional task that may not always be written out in the job summary. While writing these letters may not necessarily be an unpleasant experience, it surely takes time out of teachers' already busy schedules. Many teachers also advise or organize clubs and oversee various programs within the community. Again, although this may be an enjoyable responsibility, it is another commitment many teachers make to see us succeed.

Yet despite the endless list of jobs teachers are tasked with, they are often vilified by the media. We live within a political climate that loves to hate on teachers and undermine the importance of what they do. On top of being underpaid, teachers face rude comments from parents, people questioning their qualifications and diminishing their expertise, decisions on whether to teach certain content that could be deemed controversial, and rampant criticism of the teacher shortage. Meanwhile, they are expected to be innovative, adaptable, keep up with the changing times, while still being good teachers and carrying out all of the above responsibilities. We try to mend these issues with things like Teacher Appreciation Week, but is that really enough?

It is so easy to get caught up in our own problems, but maybe teachers are not the enemy. We have all experienced the last year together and have faced many of the same struggles. As cliche as it is, we have all been in the same boat. I am sure teachers are just as tired, if not more, than we are. Cut them a little slack, stop yourself before your third complaint of the class, maybe even say thank you. At the end of the day, I think it is fair to say that we are all trying our best, and maybe a little compassion could make it just a bit easier for all of us. Maybe collectively embracing the ups and downs of the past year, and maybe giving each other just the slightest bit of additional grace will eliminate some of the stress we face as we all get through this home stretch.

Some students, like Aimee, understand it. Some families understand it. Teachers definitely understand it. If we can get a full society to wrap support around the profession that quite literally impacts *everyone*, maybe then we can focus more on the purpose of schools and learning. Only then can we focus less on finding and keeping effective teachers who also can endure policy, staff, administration, societal, and cultural changes because the strong *teacherverance* levels will be less relevant. For now, teachers must know they are valued and feel that through the ways we treat them and the stories we tell. Teachers—I hope you know how needed you are. Thank you for persevering.

Next Steps

Thank you for reading—Let's connect!

We would love to hear how this book inspired you and/or your organization, school, or community.

Please consider the following:

Share this book with a friend, colleague, or teacher…

Bonus points for sharing this book with the teachers of your own kids and your friends who are teachers, or some teachers you had when you were in school!

Leave a review on Amazon so we can hear what you thought, and others can know it is worth their time! Simply search: *Teacherverance* on Amazon to write the review.

Reach out to share your story—https://drjenmott.com/contact/

In addition to reaching out to Jen directly via the contact form from her website, consider finding her via social media – Dr. Jen Mott on Facebook and/or @j.mott on Instagram. A private or public message about what you learned from this book would truly mean the world.

Jen reads every story and will personally respond to as many as possible as she loves connecting with educators everywhere and would love to hear about the book's impact.

Bring Jen Mott to your school or organization to speak (and juggle!), facilitate a workshop (balloon animals teaching about empathy for learners and juggling lessons on teacher perseverance, anyone?), and/or to do a book signing! https://drjenmott.com/contact/

Download your free *Teacherverance* resource on https://drjenmott.com/books/ and check out Jen's other books and/or social media channels to connect!

Acknowledgments

First and foremost, I would like to recognize the overwhelming support of my family from the beginning. The culmination of the original study on which this book is based made me a third-generation Dr. Mott, proudly following in the footsteps of both my father and his father. Coming from a family of educators has greatly impacted the heart behind this study as well as the drive and passion I have for education as a profession. My mom, dad, and brother have been by my side every step of the way, and I am grateful for their love and care for me as I pursue every major life milestone. I am also in awe of my extended family and friends, especially those who have played a huge, daily role in supporting me throughout this process. So thankful.

When I finished the original study, I knew I wanted to make it into a book so the stories of these veteran teachers would spread wider and farther and inspire an entire generation of teachers working their hardest. I quickly determined I needed help and a coach. I found this in Jake Kelfer—www.JakeKelfer.com – and the incredible Big Idea to Bestseller author community he fosters daily. This group was the right program for me and my goals, while affirming throughout the entire process by way of the leaders I met and worked with and the fellow aspiring authors I met who became friends.

The other group I have joined since the study, Heroic Public Speaking—www.heroicpublicspeaking.com – focuses on speaking for the purpose of changing lives, is led by Amy and Michael Port. Surrounding myself with a group of talented authors and inspirational speakers I admired will forever be one of the greatest gifts I have given myself and I am grateful for the community they created.

Writing a book is one big group project! There are people who made this project happen beyond these colleagues from these groups. The cover was designed by Carrie O'Neal. You can learn more about her amazing work at https://onealdesigns.com/ because she not only does special projects but also has her work in lots of different places you might even recognize (like Target, West Elm, Disney, and The MET!). She was also a school board member at one of the schools where I used to work, so she felt directly connected to the work, which I appreciated.

Then there were the original editors I worked with to help develop the concepts of this book, from a dissertation in an academic study to the book you are reading here. They are Alex Baggott-Rowe and Allison Baggott-Rowe, and they were enormously helpful in the initial edits as I transferred my thoughts from one format to the other. Even better—Alex is a local full-time teacher who does editing on the side, and Allison (www.allisonbaggottrowe.com) is a former circus performer, plus I learned about them through a fellow speaker from the other program, so I naturally felt right at home working with both of them. Networking at its finest! I finished the editing piece with Catt Editing, LLC—https://www.cattediting.com/ who was incredibly kind, helpful, encouraging, and efficient in helping get the project completed quicker than I even expected.

Tom Pesce is who you first read from at the beginning of this book. I met him through the public speaker community, and he was kind enough to write the Foreword. I wanted a teacher who was not in my study or in my Greater Cincinnati network to contribute to this work and we have a few things in common. If you check out his website—www.tompesce.com – you will quickly learn he is a full-time educator, part-time keynote speaker, *and* a magician! I will forever be grateful for his quick support of this project after just months of knowing one another. Hopefully we will meet in person one day so I can shake his hand and thank him in person while he shows me some amazing magic.

Thanks, also, to Zach Long with www.LifeAfterTeaching.com for so generously sharing his story. This immensely contributed to the necessity for this work due to the fact that he and his wife both left teaching to start a new mission. The work they do in supporting teachers as they leave the profession only exacerbates the need for the themes from this book to be lived. We are all working towards supporting teachers while continuing to impact systems and perception to better equip and motivate teachers overall.

To help the entire project come to completion, Emily Hunter-Higgins stepped in with her ability to finalize all the details. Through her efforts at https://creativesnug.com she helps authors from all over complete their projects, working with publishers, and enjoys working with the authors directly. This became a global project since she is based in the United Kingdom!

From the original study that informed this book, I would like to thank Dr. Gail F. Latta, Dr. Curtis, and Dr. Tobergte at Xavier University, who not only served on the committee but also became educators and mentors that I deeply admire and respect. Now that I work consistently for Xavier University, I am also grateful for Dr. Brett Burton, the Program

Director for Educational Administration, who has cheered me along as I teach and write. All the graduate students I have been fortunate enough to have in classes throughout this process have also offered immense support.

This book told the stories of teachers I met from the study as well as many I have personally worked with throughout my career (and/or had as my own teachers!). The career so far spans four different roles in five amazing schools in six strong school districts across two different states. Therefore, it is necessary to first thank the staff of Sycamore Community Schools, who were there with me from the beginning, as that is where I attended as a student (as a second-generation graduate and teacher) and taught later. I started my career as a long-term substitute in Mariemont City Schools and was immediately welcomed into the teaching profession with open arms and all the encouragement I needed.

The staff at Highlands High School in Fort Thomas Independent Schools cheered me along during the study and gave me the opportunity to take an incredible group of students to Spain, reinforcing my love for language, cultures, and travel mixed with education. The staff at Fairfield High School was always supportive and encouraging of my efforts toward my coursework and beginning the original research on teacher perseverance.

Most recently, the staff in Mason City Schools supported me as I crossed the finish line of the study in 2020 and the book process in the 2023–24 school year, so I appreciate their joining in my excitement as I—along with a talented leadership team—continue to lead with empathy, curiosity, and humility and support the teachers who are persevering while supporting our students and families. I would also like to thank Aimee and The Chronicle staff for allowing me to end with her contribution from their Mason student newspaper.

While I am unsure how many teacher or education books acknowledge a circus, I would be remiss to not mention the Cincinnati Circus Company—a company I have been with through my bachelor's, master's, and doctoral degrees and now becoming an author, all while being a professional juggler, balloon artist, stilt-walker, and fire performer. For nearly twenty years, it has been the most consistent job I have had and taught me about perseverance in unique, fun, and fresh ways that are unlikely in other workplaces. Particularly, I give thanks to my fellow entertainers who have encouraged me along the way. And special thanks to former classroom teacher Dave Willacker—the founder and owner of Cincinnati Circus—who has allowed my circus career to evolve with my professional educational career as he has supported my efforts toward both my doctoral degree and pursuing a professional speaking career (www. cincinnaticircus.com/jen-mott and www.DrJenMott.com).

Finally, a note for the *classroom teachers*. My heroes. Classroom teachers are an integral part of society. Personally, in Sycamore Community Schools, classroom teachers are who shaped me as an early student and who helped get me started on a new trajectory in my career, along with some mentors. Then there are the *forty-four* amazingly dedicated classroom teachers who volunteered their precious time to participate in this study. Any fall would be a challenging time for classroom teachers to engage in additional projects as they approached the end of semester. However, fall 2020 was the most challenging school year any of us have had in our careers, and I still was able to gain permission from over forty teachers representing seven of the nine districts contacted. Special thanks to the following school districts for allowing their teachers to participate in this work: Northwest Local Schools (Colerain), Fairfield City Schools, Lakota Local School District, Mason City Schools, Oak Hills Local School District, Princeton City Schools, and Sycamore Community Schools.

To the teachers who participated: It was an absolute pleasure getting to know you, hear your stories, and learn more about the *teacherverance* you possess. Thank you for your participation and for your investment in your students, colleagues, and the profession overall. And thanks to those of you who gave me updates to inform this book. It was great to hear about all you are up to. Keep up the important work!

To the teachers and administrators who read this: Our work has an invaluable impact on this world. We are fortunate to be in the business of people as we get the chance daily to impact people's lives in unique, tangible, and meaningful ways. Administrators: may you use this study to learn ways to harness *teacherverance* in your own school community and leverage the experience of veteran teachers to improve overall morale. Teachers: May you find this study to be an encouragement and gift to you as you consider ways to continue persevering in such a demanding, yet important, profession. You are not alone. Keep persevering—or better yet—keep demonstrating the *teacherverance* you possess!

Author Biography
A Doctor, a Juggler, *and* an Educator Walk into a School...

Dr. Jen Mott has been with Cincinnati Circus Company since 2006 as a juggler, stilt-walker, balloon artist, and fire performer when she also began college. Since then, she earned both her undergraduate degree in secondary education for Spanish and completed her master's program in curriculum and instruction from the University of Cincinnati. There she also had the opportunity to be part of the first ever Division I lacrosse team for UC.

In 2020, Dr. Mott earned her doctor of education degree in leadership studies at Xavier University, Cincinnati, Ohio, where she initiated her research interest on teacher perseverance. She continues to serve Xavier University as a faculty member in the educational administration program.

While Cincinnati Circus Company has been her consistent weekend and summer job since 2006, Dr. Mott has continued to serve the students, staff, and broader education community in a variety of capacities as a Spanish and Teacher of English to Speakers of Other Languages (TESOL). After classroom teaching, Dr. Mott moved into school administration and is currently a middle school administrator and athletic director in one of the largest public school districts in Ohio.

In addition to her daily duties in the community that she serves, Dr. Mott has performed at a multitude of school presentations for students and staff. She has expanded her message of capturing our full potential and saying *yes* to new opportunities in the areas of business, organizational development, entrepreneurship, and creativity. She also did a TEDx Talk regarding her "Creative Spark" of *Juggling Career and Passion* in 2023, which you can watch here: bit.ly/JMottTEDx.

In her free time, Dr. Mott can be found planning trips, booking flights, and traveling across the country and internationally, having been to as many countries as she is years old. Being a fluent Spanish speaker adds value to the Spanish-speaking countries she visits and performs in; however, she is always looking forward to more new opportunities to come since she is passionate about adventure, new experiences, cultures, and continually learning along the journey.

This book is her first of two books published around the same time. The other book is a picture book companion to *Teacherverance* called *Why Teaching?,* which tells the story of a kid who wants to be a teacher in a post-COVID-19 world even though none of the adults are encouraging them to do so. Why does this kid still want to teach? TLDR: Teachers impact all professions and people. For more, check out the full book by searching: *Why Teaching?* on Amazon and/or visiting https://drjenmott.com/books/ for updates.

Groups can work with Dr. Mott anytime they need help motivating leaders, employees, students, or parents in unique, engaging ways that incorporate juggling or balloon storytelling from a professional in the field through workshops, keynote speaking, and anything else they can dream up together! Reach out anytime: https://drjenmott. com/contact/. Turns out—the Doctor, the Juggler, and the Educator are all the same person, and she wants to meet you!

Endnotes

[1] Leib Sutcher, Linda Darling-Hammond, and Desiree Carver-Thomas, "A coming crisis in teaching? Teacher supply, demand, and shortages in the U.S.," Learning Policy Institute, September 15, 2016, https://learningpolicyinstitute.org/product/coming-crisis-teaching.

[2] Carver-Thomas & Darling-Hammond, 2019.

[3] Sutcher, Darling-Hammond, and Carver-Thomas, "A coming crisis in teaching? Teacher supply, demand, and shortages in the U.S.," 3.

[4] Madeline Will, "10 Ways the Teaching Profession Has Changed Over the Past 10 Years," Education Week, edweek.org, December 12, 2019, https://www.edweek.org/teaching-learning/10-ways-the-teaching-profession-has-changed-over-the-past-10-years/2019/12.

[5] We Are Teachers Staff, "These 2023 Teacher Shortage Statistics Prove We Need to Fix This Profession," weareteachers.com, June 27, 2023, https://www.weareteachers.com/teacher-shortage-statistics/.

[6] Carver-Thomas and Darling-Hammond, "The trouble with teacher turnover."

[7] "The Role of Principals in Addressing Teacher Shortages" (research brief), Learning Policy Institute, 2017, https://learningpolicyinstitute.org/product/role-principals-addressing-teacher-shortages-brief.

[8] Bo Shen, Nate McCaughtry, Jeffreu Martin, Alex Garn, Noel Kulik, and Mariane Fahlman, "The relationship between teacher burnout and student motivation," *British Journal of Educational Psychology 85*, no. 4 (2015): 12, https://psycnet.apa.org/doi/10.1111/bjep.12089.

[9] Carver-Thomas and Darling-Hammond, "The trouble with teacher turnover," 16.

[10] Elizabeth Bettini, Allison F. Gilmour, Thomas O. Williams, and Bonnie Billingsley, "Predicting Special and General Educators'

Teacherverance

Intent to Continue Teaching Using Conservation of Resources Theory," *Exceptional Children 86*, no. 3 (2019): 310, https://doi.org/10.1177/0014402919870464.

[11] Bonnie Billingsley and Elizabeth Bettini, "Special Education Teacher Attrition and Retention: A Review of the Literature," *Review of Educational Research 89*, no. 5 (2019): 698, https://doi.org/10.3102/0034654319862495.

[12] Petula Dvorak, "There's no shortage of teachers. We've just driven them out of schools," *The Washington Post,* August 8, 2022, https://www.washingtonpost.com/dc-md-va/2022/08/08/teacher-shortage-schools-shootings-culture-wars/.

[13] Annie Duke, *Quit* (New York, NY: Portfolio, 2022).

[14] Dr. Julia Keller, *Quitting* (New York, NY: Balance, 2023).

[15] David Bell and Earl Thomas, "A Mentoring Process to Support Teachers' Growth and Retention," *Academic Leadership: The Online Journal 5*, no. 3 (2007): 2, http://doi.org/10.58809/LOVY7125.

[16] Sheila Bassoppo-Moyo, "Attrition—A Sign of Leadership Problems," *Academic Leadership: The Online Journal, 8*, no. 2 (2010): 35–36, http://doi.org/10.58809/FMLS3553.

[17] Vicki Luther and Laila J. Richman, "Teacher Attrition: Listening to Teachers to Find a Solution," *Academic Leadership: The Online Journal 7,* no. 4 (2009): 29–32, http://dx.doi.org/10.58809/RQEG4177.

[18] Melanie Tait, "Resilience as a Contributor to Novice Teacher Success, Commitment, and Retention," *Teacher Education Quarterly 35* (Fall 2008): 70.

[19] Luther and Richman, "Teacher Attrition: Listening to Teachers to Find a Solution."

[20] Deborah S. Yost, "Reflection and Self-Efficacy: Enhancing the Retention of Qualified Teachers from a Teacher Education Perspective," *Teacher Education Quarterly 33,* no. 4 (Fall 2006): 73.

[21] Yost, "Reflection and Self-Efficacy," 73.

[22] Tait, "Resilience as a Contributor to Novice Teacher Success," 70.

23 Becky L. Bobek, "Teacher Resiliency: A Key to Career Longevity," *The Clearing House 75*, no. 4 (2002): 203, http://dx.doi.org/10.1080/00098650209604932.

24 Desiree Carver-Thomas and Linda Darling-Hammond, *Teacher turnover: Why it matters and what we can do about it* (Palo Alto, CA: Learning Policy Institute, 2017).

25 John Schmitt and Katherine DeCourcy, "The pandemic has exacerbated a long-standing national shortage of teachers," Economic Policy Institute, December 6, 2022, https://www.epi.org/publication/shortage-of-teachers/.

26 Tim Walker, "NEA: Real Solutions, Not Band-Aids, Will Fix Educator Shortage," neaToday, October 4, 2022, https://www.nea.org/nea-today/all-news-articles/nea-real-solutions-not-band-aids-will-fix-educator-shortage.

27 Carver-Thomas and Darling-Hammond, "The trouble with teacher turnover."

28 Jerold C. Osbourn, "Factors That Influence K-8 Educators in Regard to Teacher Retention," *Dissertations 128* (Fall 2018), https://digitalcommons.lindenwood.edu/dissertations/128?utm_source=digitalcommons.lindenwood.edu%2Fdissertations%2F128&utm_medium=PDF&utm_campaign=PDFCoverPages.

29 Tara Kini and Anne Podolsky, "Does Teaching Experience Increase Teacher Effectiveness? A Review of the Research," Learning Policy Institute, June 2016, https://learningpolicyinstitute.org/sites/default/files/product-files/Teaching_Experience_Report_June_2016.pdf.

30 Carver-Thomas and Darling-Hammond, *Teacher turnover.*

31 Laura Meckler, "For many home-schoolers, parents are no longer doing the teaching," *The Washington Post,* August 17, 2023, https://www.washingtonpost.com/education/interactive/2023/homeschooling-microschools-pods-esa-vouchers/.

32 Angela Duckworth, *Grit: The Power of Passion and Perseverance* (New York, NY: Scribner, 2016).

[33] Jonathan Kozol, *Savage Inequalities: Children in America's Schools* (New York, NY: Crown, 2012).

[34] Ron Clark, *Move Your Bus: An Extraordinary New Approach to Accelerating Success in Work and Life* (New York, NY: Simon & Schuster, 2015).

[35] George Couros, Dr. Jody Carrington, et al., *Because of a Teacher: Stories of the Past to Inspire the Future of Education* (Canterbury, UK: Impress, 2021).

[36] "Holding teaching up as a higher calling is how we keep teachers down," *The Boston Globe,* updated February 7, 2023, https://www.bostonglobe.com/2023/02/07/opinion/holding-teaching-up-higher-calling-is-how-we-keep-teachers-down/.

[37] Chip Heath and Dan Heath, *The Power of Moments: Why Certain Experiences Have Extraordinary Impact* (New York, NY: Simon and Schuster, 2017).

[38] Aimee Picchi and Sanvi Bangalore, "Education was once the No. 1 major for college students. Now it's an afterthought," CBS News, cbsnews.com, July 17, 2023, https://www.cbsnews.com/news/education-majors-colleges-decline-teacher-pay/; Michael T. Nietzel, "The Five Most Significant Ten-Year Trends in College Majors," *Forbes,* forbes.com, July 24, 2022, https://www.forbes.com/sites/michaeltnietzel/2022/07/24/the-five-most-significant-ten-year-trends-in-college-majors/?sh=6a2071d4350f; "Table 322.10. Bachelor's degrees conferred by postsecondary institutions, by field of study: Selected academic years, 1970-71 through 2020-21," National Center for Education Statistics, *Digest of Education Statistics,* 2022, https://nces.ed.gov/programs/digest/d22/tables/dt22_322.10.asp.

[39] Aimee Liu, "Give Your Teachers Some Grace," *The Chronicle,* May 12, 2023, https://mhschronicle.com/give-your-teachers-some-grace/.

Made in United States
Orlando, FL
21 October 2024

52955420R00087